Your Guide to Effective Publications:

A Handbook for Campus Publications Professionals

by Kelvin J. Arden and William J. Whalen

Council for Advancement and Support of Education

ISBN 0-89964-282-9

Printed in the United States of America.

In 1974, the American Alumni Council (founded in 1913) and the American College Public Relations Association (founded in 1917) merged to become the Council for Advancement and Support of Education (CASE).

Today, approximately 2,900 colleges, universities, and independent elementary and secondary schools in the U.S. and 20 other countries belong to CASE. This makes CASE the largest nonprofit 501(c)(3) education association in terms of institutional membership. Representing the member institutions in CASE are more than 13,000 individual professionals in institutional advancement.

Nonprofit education-related organizations such as hospitals, museums, libraries, cultural or performing arts groups, public radio and television stations, or foundations established for public elementary and secondary schools may affiliate with CASE as Educational Associates. Commercial firms that serve the education field may affiliate as Subscribers.

CASE's mission is to advance understanding and support of education for the benefit of society. Central to its mission are its member colleges, universities, and independent schools. CASE fulfills this mission by providing services to beginning, mid-level, and senior advancement professionals; direct services to member institutions; and public affairs programs that bond higher education to the public interest.

CASE offers books, videotapes, and focus issues of the award-winning monthly magazine, CURRENTS, to professionals in institutional advancement. The books cover topics in alumni administration, communications and marketing, fund raising, management, and student recruitment. For a copy of the catalog, write to CASE RESOURCES, Suite 400, 11 Dupont Circle, Washington, DC 20036-1207. For more information about CASE programs and services, call (202) 328-5900.

Cover illustration by Michael David Brown
Copyediting by Susan Hunt

Council for Advancement and Support of Education
Suite 400, 11 Dupont Circle, Washington, DC 20036

Contents

Foreword   i
Peter McE. Buchanan

Preface   iii
Kelvin J. Arden
William J. Whalen

1. Communicating Through Publications   1

2. Organizing the Publications Office   7

3. Editing and Writing Techniques   19

4. Buying Composition and Printing   27

5. The Catalog   39

6. Recruiting and Career Materials   49

7. Publications for Fund Raising   57

8. Direct Mail   67

9. Building an Annual Report   77

10. Handbooks   85

11. Newsletters   91

12. Internal Communications   95

13. Special Purpose Publications   103

14. Using Photos and Photographers   109

15. Art and Design   115

16. Stretching Your Publications Dollar   123

17. The New Technology   129
    Kelvin J. Arden

18. From Composing Sticks to Computers: An Afterword   135
    William J. Whalen

Appendix: How to Break into Print   141

About the Authors   157

Bibliography   159

Index   165

Foreword

C ASE is delighted to present *Your Guide to Effective Publications: A Handbook for Campus Publications Professionals.* This new, revised and updated edition of CASE's classic on publications will serve beginners and experienced professionals for years to come.

In 1965 when Kel Arden and Bill Whalen wrote the first edition of this book, there was very little available in print to help a college or university carry out its publications responsibilities. In the 1960s, with the wave of baby boomers on their way to college, *Effective Publications for Colleges and Universities* was an instant success. (It wasn't published by CASE, of course, as this organization was still just an idea in the minds of some people at the American College Public Relations Association and the American Alumni Council, its predecessor organizations.)

In 1978, when the authors decided to update and revise their book, CASE was pleased to publish it as one of the earliest volumes in our new booklist. Printed from typed copy and distributed in a looseleaf notebook, *Effective Publications* was, once again, an immediate hit.

Now, in 1991, *Your Guide to Effective Publications* was edited at a computer terminal, typeset in-house from copy on a floppy disk, and printed by offset lithography. Nevertheless, the authors' original message has not been changed: Our college and university publications can be—*must* be—better.

Whether you are at the forefront of the computer revolution or are reluctant to enter the modern age, this book poses the questions and provides the answers that can make your life in the publications office easier and more productive. The basics remain the same: No matter how "high-tech" the process that puts the words onto the page, the words themselves must be carefully chosen and carefully edited or they will fail in their purpose—to persuade, to inform, to explain—in short, to communicate.

Peter McE. Buchanan
CASE President
April 1991

Preface

Every college and university in the country maintains a publications and periodicals program. For some institutions this may consist of the catalog, an alumni periodical, and a few dozen brochures and leaflets; for a large university this program may embrace hundreds of publications of all types and a seven-figure budget. One institution may have organized a complete editorial office with editors, graphic designers, writers, production coordinators, photographers, compositors, and proofreaders. Another may assign editorial responsibilities to the information director or the assistant to the president.

For many years not much was available in book form to help the college or university, large or small or in between, carry out its publications responsibility. *Composing Sticks and Mortar Boards* by Earl Schenck Miers came out in 1941 and has long since been out of print. To try to fill this void, the authors wrote *Effective Publications for Colleges and Universities,* which was published by Balt Publishers in 1965. The Council for Advancement and Support of Education (CASE) published a revised edition in 1978.

Since then other books have been published that deal with one or another aspect of college publications; we have tried to list most of them in the bibliography. Rapid changes in typesetting and printing technology; student recruiting methods; fund-raising techniques; and marketing strategies prompted the authors to prepare this completely revised and updated edition, *Your Guide to Effective Publications: A Handbook for Campus Publications Professionals.*

We have tried to distill more than 70 years of combined experience as publications directors at several universities. This handbook does not pretend to cover every possible publication. We chose to concentrate on those areas in which we have had working experience; we decided to bypass such publication categories as technical reports, alumni magazines, and student publications.

Special thanks go to Virginia Carter Smith, CASE senior vice president for operations, who nurtured this project and offered innumerable valuable suggestions. The authors would also like to thank CASE Book Editor Susan Hunt for her contributions to the organization and editing of this book.

Kelvin J. Arden
William J. Whalen

Chapter 1

Communicating Through Publications

Each year the nation's 3,400 colleges and universities issue millions of printed pieces: catalogs, newsletters, magazines, reports, brochures, posters, directories, guidance booklets, programs, books, and other publications. These institutions spend at least $400 million a year on composition and printing alone.

No institution maintains the same stable of publications as another. Some small colleges find their needs satisfied by a few dozen publications, while others set up production systems to keep track of the hundreds of printed pieces bearing their institution's imprint. Annual budgets range from $20,000 to over $1 million.

The rising threshold of attention

Those who guide the destinies of these institutions have increasingly come to realize that publications are the most efficient and reliable way to reach specific publics. College administrators have not abandoned the mass media—the daily newspapers, radio, and television. They know, however, that there are certain built-in limitations to the use of these media by higher education. The situation will get worse, not better. The sociologists and journalism researchers attribute this to the rising threshold of attention.

In most villages and small towns, the weekly or daily newspaper will publish an obituary for every resident who dies. The press will also dutifully record the vital statistics of the living: birth, graduation, engagement, marriage, promotions, perhaps even visits to the next city.

In the larger communities, those who have gone beyond must have distinguished themselves by good deeds or bad before the editor will assign an obituary. Of course, the business office will be happy to sell a classified ad listing the name of the deceased, survivors, the funeral home, and the schedule for the wake and burial service.

By the time we reach the metropolitan newspapers, only millionaires, gangsters, and celebrities rate an obit. In New York and Chicago, hundreds of people die every day but only a handful get even a few inches of type.

This situation reflects the age in which we live. Seventy-five years ago in a far less complex world, newspapers reported not only the death but the minor achievements of most citizens. In the 1990s the routine events in the lives of average people no longer claim column inches.

What does this mean for the college and university public relations program? Although the number of publicity writers may double or triple and the copy machines work night and day shifts, the chances that an important news article from campus will get respectable coverage in the daily press are becoming smaller and smaller every year. Beyond the interest radius of the campus, a virtual news blackout is pierced only by coverage of athletic events and an occasional student demonstration, drug bust, or fraternity stunt.

We are not suggesting that institutions abandon their publicity efforts or ignore the mass media. But times have changed. The mass media are just that—newspapers and other media that are meant to appeal to every educational, social, and cultural group in the U.S. today. They serve up a daily dish of news, horoscopes, advice to the lovelorn, comics, sports, gossip, cheesecake, political columnists, and so on. Space is limited, and editors ration the amount of hard news from such fields as science, education, and religion.

Not only must the average college or university compete for the tiny proportion of column inches devoted to higher education, but it cannot control the presentation of its message even if the news release is picked up. It cannot determine the story's position in the paper, its final length, its editing, its headline, or when it will appear. These decisions remain in the hands of copy editors who may be sympathetic, indifferent, or even downright hostile to the institution or to higher education.

And too often what space the media give to higher education is devoted to the trivial—photos of shapely cheerleaders, gag shots of Frisbee contests, and scandals involving professors and/or students. The public's opinion of higher education too often has been formed by such trivia, which presents college as a round of dances, fraternity parties, football games, sex, and shenanigans.

You can't blame the newspaper editors. Most of them do a first-rate, conscientious job, and all are hard pressed by space and time requirements. They must keep in mind that they are not editing a daily edition of the *Atlantic* or *Harper's*. Some have actually increased the number of higher education stories in their newspapers, but the papers themselves are physically larger, and the chance that any one reader will spot the story and read it remains slim.

The forces that call for a reevaluation of old-time publicity techniques cannot be controlled by any one college or university or even by all of them together. They cannot be altered by persuading a few editors to boost their educational coverage. They are the product of the population explosion, urbanization, newspaper economics, complex government, and human psychology.

What we have said about the press applies equally to radio and television. In most cities "formula" radio is the rule, i.e., music, weather, news, sports. The educational radio and TV stations reach only a minority of the American people. With a few exceptions, what universities are able to bag prime time for educational TV programs? Radio and TV are controlled by commercial advertisers who in turn are guided chiefly by the ratings system. A college or university can spend a fortune to develop radio and TV programs that will make a mighty small splash.

If college and universities rely on the mass media to relay their messages, they will be disappointed because the mass audience has almost vanished. It has been replaced by innumerable subaudiences that must be reached by specialized media. For example, not too many years ago television was dominated by the major networks; today cable offers dozens of channels, and TV sets come wired for 120 channels. *Look* magazine has died, but hundreds of specialized magazines have taken its place. How much educational information do you hear today on talk shows, Top 40 stations, or country and western programs?

The facts of life in the 1990s boil down to this: If an institution wants to prepare its own message, determine its format, and pick its audience, it cannot rely on the mass media. It must depend on printed publications to do this job.

The need for control, professionals

Colleges that have recognized the facts of communications life today and have examined their present publications budgets have sometimes been surprised. They have discovered that when everything is counted, they are already spending far more money for printed material and the editorial and design work that goes into it than they do for the rest of their public relations program put together. And yet in too many cases this expensive and extensive publications program lacks centralized direction, purpose, and professional competence.

The number of publications offices has grown during the past 40 years, but some institutions, which long ago centralized purchasing, admissions counseling, publicity, housing management, and the like, continue to divide responsibility for publications among a number of different campus offices.

Academic departments feel free to write brochures, the registrar issues the catalog, the personnel office tries its hand at a newsletter, the admissions director gets out guidance pamphlets, and so on. These institutions have failed to realize that this haphazard arrangement will not produce publications that accurately reflect the institution and interpret its needs to the public.

Oddly enough, some colleges and universities that preach the gospel of creativity and innovation seem content with pedestrian publications that are poorly written, edited, designed, and printed.

No college president should expect the same results from amateur writers, amateur editors, amateur photographers, and amateur designers that he or she should expect from professionals. Unfortunately, too many college administrators fail to recognize their amateur standing in some of these specializations. Administrators who would never attempt to do the work of an architect or a composer try to write and design publications that will compete successfully for the attention of busy men and women. It can't be done.

Even though the message of these publications may be an important one, expressed with honesty and enthusiasm, this is often not enough. The average American is assaulted by as many as 270 advertising appeals every day of the year. Opinion molders, professional people, politicians, and philanthropists stand well above this average. The do-it-yourself college publication will not win the battle for interest in this type of competition.

This does not mean that Madison Avenue's wildest slogans and brashest schemes should find shelter in ivy-covered walls. It does mean that John and Jane Doe now expect that material from an institution seeking their dollars or their interest will reflect certain standards of writing, typography, illustration, and printing.

Not everyone can play the piano or sing on key or paint a picture. Not everyone can write, organize material, design a booklet. These abilities come with training and practice. Many institutions have recognized this by appointing university editors or directors of publications. Those jacks-of-all-trades who can design a brochure, write a news release, produce a TV program, wheedle a gift from a corporation, deliver a speech, counsel new students, and set up an exhibit cannot compete successfully with colleagues who enter these areas with technical as well as general backgrounds and devote their full energies to mastering these arts.

We may all read the little stories our children compose in grade school and admire their drawings, but do we show the same interest in the efforts of our neighbor's children? Many people you hope to interest and inform with your publications share one attitude: indifference. They are indifferent to higher education and its goals and, unfortunately, they may well be indifferent to your particular institution as well. At the most, they may give your appeal a priority well below that of a dozen others they receive. You will not reach them by publications that reveal only sincerity and good will.

While a small liberal arts college, a two-year college, or a regional campus might assign publication responsibilities to someone who wears several other hats, a large university might employ 20 to 25 people in its publications office.

For the larger institution, the volume of publications demonstrates the need for professional publications specialists. These professionals may work with the general public relations staff, or they may direct separate editorial offices.

For the smaller institution it may be out of the question to hire someone to handle nothing but printed material. We suggest, however, that every college that lacks a publications office or a full-time editor make a comprehensive survey of its printing requirements. If some of these colleges add up all their printing bills, editorial hours, and the publications they need but never have the time and the staff to prepare, they may find that they already have more than enough work for a full-time editor. This may well be the case for any college that has more than 1,000 students.

Since printing absorbs such a large share of the college public relations budget, a college or university can hire a competent editor who knows the printing business and get back in savings every penny of his or her salary. An alert editor with professional qualifications should not find it difficult to cut the printing bills by 20 percent the first year over the former haphazard and decentralized system.

This person should know how to write printing specifications; how to select the right typesetters and printers to bid on jobs; how to save money by choosing one paper stock or one format over more expensive ones; how to comply with U.S. Postal Service regulations; and how to negotiate with free-lance writers, designers, illustrators, and photographers. He or she should know the basic principles of legibility and readability.

The role of institutional publications

In addition to those publications that we might term "promotional," an institution must produce those that contribute to efficient management. Here, too, the publications professional can demonstrate his or her usefulness. An accurate and complete staff and student directory issued early in the fall semester can facilitate campus communications. A comprehensive handbook for staff members can answer dozens of questions that would otherwise call for personal letters.

Effective publications can help an institution face the problems associated with the lower birth rate of the population and the need for additional voluntary support. As enrollments stabilize, colleges and universities need publications that will help them get their share of the dwindling freshman classes. Personal cultivation and the mass media are important in any campaign for freshmen, funds, and friends, but the printed piece remains an essential channel to reach prospective students, alumni, parents, townspeople, taxpayers, church constituencies, corporations, foundations, legislators, and other publics. While these publications should strive to put the institution's best foot forward, they should never distort reality or make unwarranted claims.

People who put out publications usually want to do more than provide information. They want the readers to take some sort of action, form an opinion, purchase the product, contribute money. That means that publications should persuade as well as inform. To get the kind of response you want, you will need to use the techniques of marketing.

Publications already represent one of the largest—if not *the* largest—public relations expenditure. Colleges and universities are increasingly turning away from the mass media to publications targeted for specific audiences. Newspapers may be printing more education news and features, but individual institutions must share this space with every level of education, with every other institution, with every other news item. As the threshold of attention goes up, often only the outstanding, bizarre, or gigantic can claim space in the daily press, radio, and TV.

To reach the many publics of the college or university—alumni, faculty and staff, donors and potential donors, legislators, parents, students, church supporters—the institution must rely on the well-executed, dignified publication directed to the desk or mailbox of the intended recipient.

Chapter 2

Organizing the Publications Office

If each department or division is to design its own printing, each without adequate supervision or general theme, then the result can be only a hodgepodge (and, indeed, this explains precisely what is happening in many institutions). There should be one office, directed by a competent person, through which all institutional printing should pass, and it should become the function of this office to design the printing, write the specifications, and supervise the various operations of manufacture (Earl Schenck Miers, *Composing Sticks and Mortar Boards,* 1941).

The purpose of any office is to do a job better and more efficiently than can be done by scattered individuals. The job of a publications office is to produce publications for a college or university in the best possible manner. To do the job, an office must assemble experts and must establish procedures. This is just as true for the one-person shop as it is for the large office made up of 15 to 25 publications specialists.

An effective publications office should conserve the institution's budget by getting the most out of every printing dollar. By employing the best possible personnel in editing and design, it should ensure the accuracy and quality of its publications. By concentrating control of all the publications in one office, even a small college can hire some full-time professional people, instead of relying entirely upon part-time help.

The editor

The first staff member to look for in the publications office is a person with good creative editorial skills. Such a person is not always easy to find. Good artwork can be purchased outside. Good design, good printing, and good photography are readily available. But a person who can edit, organize, and write clearly is a person of the utmost value to any publications program.

Some might advise that the most important staff member should be a computer technician. This is certainly something for publications directors to consider seriously in these days of desktop publishing and preprogrammed publication design. However, even though a machine may correct your spelling and make an accurate page layout, the first and most important element is still an idea—and the words that make it come alive.

There are few colleges in the country that are so small that they can't afford to have one good publications person. If your institution produces only 20 or 30 pieces of printing a year, you won't need a large full-time staff. A number of commercial firms provide expert help in design, layout, and photography; in some cases, they will even write and edit copy. However, whatever outside help your office uses, all basic editorial decisions should be made on campus.

The designer

After the creative editor, the next most valuable member of the staff is the graphic designer. This person is not necessarily an artist as well, nor are all artists good designers. A competent publications designer should know type—its readability as well as its visual and psychological impact. The designer must also be familiar with today's advanced electronic typesetting systems. Many publications offices now meet most of their type needs in-house. Some elements of printing have not changed significantly. Designers still need a solid working knowledge of paper, ink, and the various printing processes that combine to create graphic effects.

Since most promotional brochures are more than 60 percent visual material, designers must also be expert at selecting and using photographs. An office is fortunate if a designer can also fill in as an on-the-spot campus photographer, but you should not expect your designer to also be a gifted artist, able to produce a line sketch, a cartoon, or a portrait of your wealthiest trustee.

Whether your office includes a full-time designer should depend on the workload. You may only need a part-time person for design work. If your campus is located near a large metropolitan center, you will have a choice of good free-lance designers. For a small or medium-sized college, this may be the best solution.

The copy editor

In addition to a creative editor and graphic designer, you should consider hiring a copy editor. A copy editor is both a rewriter and a stylist—one who loves to work with details and is enthusiastic about tracking down esoteric words and painstaking about making sure that the facts are accurate and the grammar correct.

The day-to-day assignments of a copy editor include the following:

• editing: The copy editor reads all incoming copy for style and accuracy; resolves all points of style and does necessary minor rephrasing without consulting the writer; catches errors in fact and informs the writer of the error and the changes in copy that are indicated; informs the director or the editor of any major defects in writing or organization; does the necessary rewriting and reorganizing and has the revisions approved by the writer.

• proofing: Proofreading is done on hard copy (proof from a printer or a print-out from a word-processor) or on a computer terminal. Proofreading copy on a computer terminal before it is set in type or printed out saves time, money, and paper, but it also puts an added burden for accuracy and editorial judgment on the copy editor.

• critiquing: The copy editor evaluates for content, style, accuracy, and organization any publication assigned by the director and rewrites if necessary.

• writing: The copy editor writes any features or brochures assigned by the publications director.

One of the most important functions of a publications office is to control the style and accuracy of the institution's official documents such as catalogs and annual reports. This can only be done efficiently in one place by an editor and an editorial staff who consistently enforce good style and good grammar and who check the accuracy of factual information.

Almost all publications call for a team effort, and every team should have a captain; that person is called the editor or project manager. The editor must coordinate the efforts of the writer, the graphic designer, the photographer, and the illustrator; if the editor has final responsibility for the publication, he or she must also have the final authority to accept or reject the various elements that go into the job.

Other staff members

Depending upon the volume and type of work your office does, you might need a proofreader, production manager, and a writer.

If you have a steady flow of editorial work, a full-time or part-time proofreader might well be an indispensable staff member. A good proofreader, while in some jeopardy from an electronic dictionary and a thesaurus, can still save you not only unnecessary composition costs but public embarrassment as well. The proofreader stands as a final guard against inaccurate figures, faulty punctuation, and misspelled trustees' names.

The publications production manager may serve as expediter, recordkeeper, printing buyer, and technical adviser. This job calls for someone well-versed in the art of the possible. How to get the job done on time, within the budget, and to the satisfaction of the "customer" is the main task of the production manager.

If your office is responsible for the content of important promotional and fund-raising brochures, a staff writer is not a luxury but a necessity. Finding and organizing sources of information within a complex institution is often an almost impossible task for the outside or free-lance writer. A competent staff writer has a distinct advantage in locating background material and in accurately reflecting official attitudes and policies.

Setting publications priorities

To get the most from good personnel, an office staff needs to have a firm and clearcut definition of its responsibilities and the procedures to implement them. Every publications office must set priorities, and these will vary from one institution to another.

For example, a private university that accepts one out of every four qualified applicants might put development publications at the top of its list. For another institution, student recruitment materials would come first. Internal and external communications and public relations would appear on most priority listings. A formal ranking of priorities, approved by the president and/or the officer who supervises the publications office, puts the office in sync with the goals of the institution. It also allows the publications director to turn down projects in the busy season if they rank too low on the list of priorities.

Publications office responsibilities

There are four main areas of responsibility in which a publications office should function: editorial, budgetary, production, and distribution.

Editorial. Perhaps the most important function of the publications office is its editorial responsibility. Briefly, this responsibility has two parts:

1. *Determination of suitability of copy for content and style.* This publications responsibility is often one of the most difficult to enforce. It requires great tact and diplomacy on the part of the publications officer. There are times when you have to tell the dean or the president that his or her copy is not suitable for publication in its present form. You need to do this in such a way that the person will be willing to rewrite the copy or approve someone else's rewrite so that it will be suitable for the audience for which it is designed. If you do this skillfully, the original writer will be left feeling that you have helped bring out the best in the original copy—and you won't get fired!

2. *Review and styling of all copy* before *it is set in type.* This is particularly important for copy that originates in other offices or departments. For example, course descriptions for the college catalog often vary widely in content, length, and style. Establishing firm editorial guidelines before copy is submitted will pay off in fewer headaches later. For regularly issued publications such as catalogs, copy is frequently stored from year to year in computer systems and requires only a quick revision before printing. The publications office is also responsible for maintaining the accuracy and uniformity of general institutional information, particularly in a quasi-legal document such as the college catalog. On every campus there will

be students who will be looking for loopholes in the language you have used in the catalog—to escape requirements for a degree or to get around campus regulations. The language used in the catalog should be as precise and accurate as you can make it.

Budgetary. The budgetary responsibility of a publications office should start with the initial planning of a publication. The director of publications should be involved in the initial decision for allocation of funds. In this way, publications professionals have a voice in what the publications will eventually look like.

The publications office is responsible for the following:

• preliminary planning of annual printing budgets and schedules for the various schools or departments;

• checking of all printing to make sure that it will stay within budget limitations;

• review of all printing bills against estimates and finished work; and

• review of long-term budgetary commitments.

Since advance publication planning is essential to living within a budget and maintaining production schedules, most editorial offices that handle a volume of work use preliminary planning sheets. These simple forms must be filled out by any department or individual ordering a publication. The planning sheet clarifies the purposes and determines the need for a particular printed piece. (See the next page for a sample planning sheet.)

Production. The publications office's production responsibilities include:

• approving the design, typography, and artwork of all college printing;

• providing consultation on matters of general publication design;

• establishing and maintaining a schedule of printing for annual publications such as catalogs, alumni and general magazines, and annual reports; and

• approving the quality of finished work and maintaining a complete file of all college publications.

Production also includes purchasing—the buying of printing. Purchasing includes two elements:

• soliciting estimates and bids for printing; and

• originating purchase orders for printing, illustrative materials, and mailing services.

Chapter 4 discusses purchasing in greater detail.

Distribution. The responsibility for distribution of all printed materials includes the following:

• supervising outside mailings and internal distribution;

• securing special mailing lists for promotional materials;

• maintaining permanent mailing lists for publications that are distributed at regular intervals;

• seeking out and distributing information on mailing procedures, methods, and equipment;

• checking all mailings to ensure maximum economy and compliance with postal regulations; and

• keeping publications inventory and mailing records.

**Office of Publications
Planning Guide/Schedule**

Date _____

Title _____   Requested delivery date _____

School/Dept. _____   Actual delivery date _____

Contact _____   Phone _____

Campus address _____   Account No. _____

Editor _____   Designer _____

☐ New publication   Will publication be reissued? _____   How soon? _____

☐ Reprint   Quantity _____   Audience _____

☐ Revision   Budget _____   Envelopes and/or other materials _____

Special instructions:

Presentation:	**Schedule and log**	**Date due**	**Date done**	**Ok'd**
☐ Straight text	Mss. submitted	_____	_____	_____
☐ Photos (No.) _____	Editing	_____	_____	_____
Source _____	Design	_____	_____	_____
☐ Charts (No.) _____	Comp. bids requested	_____	_____	_____
☐ Drawings (No.) _____	Comp. bids received	_____	_____	_____
Format:	Printing bids requested	_____	_____	_____
☐ Booklet	Printing bids received	_____	_____	_____
☐ Self cover	Form 12/work order rec'd	_____	_____	_____
☐ Separate cover	Mss. to typesetter	_____	_____	_____
☐ Leaflet	Galleys received	_____	_____	_____
☐ Poster	Photographs	_____	_____	_____
☐ Other _____	Galleys proofread	_____	_____	_____
_____	Illustrations	_____	_____	_____
Size (No. pages) _____	Proofs returned	_____	_____	_____
☐ 4 x 9	Repro type received	_____	_____	_____
☐ 5½ x 8½	Paste-up	_____	_____	_____
☐ 6 x 9	Paste-up to printer	_____	_____	_____
☐ 8½ x 11	Page proof	_____	_____	_____
☐ Other _____	Delivery	_____	_____	_____

Comments:

Deliver to: _____

    (Individual)   **(Room)**   **(Bldg.)**

Job envelope copy: white
Editor's copy: canary
Designer's copy: pink
Client's copy: goldenrod

12

The importance of centralization

More often than not, the business of putting out the printed material that represents an institution is spread among a dozen or more departments with no attempt at planned budgeting, cost or quality control, or a coordinated system of graphics. No wonder management in this area of communications has been so scattered and ineffective since this one area alone usually accounts for a greater expenditure of money than all other areas of public relations or communications.

One of the most difficult operations in publications management is gathering enough authority in all the areas where authority is necessary to do an adequate job. For more than 20 years, a large midwestern university has benefited from an effective publications office, headed by a manager with the title of university editor. Several years ago, this office issued a Printing and Publications Policies and Procedures statement.

The introduction to this statement reads as follows:

> A body of policies and procedures governing printing and publications should be adopted in the interest of improving quality, effecting economies, establishing more uniform practices, and providing better service to departments, colleges, and the university. These policies and procedures are not to take from departments or individuals that authority over publications which stems from professional knowledge and competency.

The last sentence is of particular interest since it hints at the problems that almost inevitably arise when you are dealing with professors who are acknowledged experts in their field and may be reluctant to admit your greater expertise in the publications arena.

Publications' place in the institutional hierarchy

Where should the publications office be placed administratively? A few years ago, a survey of college and university printing and publishing practices showed that there is no well-established policy in the organizational position of publications services. Publications offices come in many shapes and sizes and are called by many different names.

The publications office may operate under a director of public relations, a director for university relations, or a vice president.

Wherever the office fits in the institutional hierarchy, the president of the institution or a delegated officer should be in a position to determine policy regarding the styling and quality of the publications. Most good publications programs are the result of one person's good sense, good taste, and strong convictions. Where policy decisions affecting copy and design are spread over a number of deans or several vice presidents, the resulting publications may have a chop-suey effect with no unifying thread and widely varying quality. This is not to say that every publication you produce should look the same. They could have a family resemblance, but publications designed to do different jobs need not look the same. An annual report should not look the same as a brochure for summer sessions, although it certainly could have the same general design feeling—a clean, open approach, for example.

Most major corporations and some universities have established graphic design systems that control the quality and look of all printed material. Bradbury Thompson, an internationally recognized designer and graphic arts innovator, has suggested a plan based upon quality of production and simplicity of design. Thompson's approach to college publications combines a clean and uncluttered style with the highest standards of graphic production. In a talk to college editors, Thompson said:

> In the case of catalogs, letterheads, and announcements, only one type should be used. This plan could afford such virtues as economy, consistency, and quality of both large and small printed work. It could be achieved with a concise manual such as we find used by large industrial corporations that have many departments and divisions. The typeface selected could reflect the historical and academic character of the university.

Some institutions have established a publications advisory committee or policy board. No new promotional publication is planned and printed without its OK. If these boards or committees are kept small and if they consist of individuals with practical experience in promotion and with an active interest in good quality printing, writing, and design, they can be most helpful. However, a committee that includes a representative of every academic department or school may wind up as a debating society with everyone trying to put across personal ideas on typography, layout, and even printing. Such a committee would hinder rather than help.

Of more value to your publications program than a standing committee may be a "working" review committee called together infrequently to take a close look at all publications procedures. Such a review committee should represent the entire institution rather than individual departments, and it might deal with the following topics:

- analysis of the purposes, costs, and methods of distribution of publications;
- survey of methods of preparation, production schedules, quantity determination;
- study of possible common standards of typography and format as they may be related to economy or increased effectiveness;
- analysis of requests for publications, methods of fulfilling requests, and inventory controls;
- review of developments in publications at other colleges and universities;
- classification of publication uses—promotional, informational, archival, etc.— and consideration of the most effective and economical ways to combine or separate such uses; and
- review of "empty spaces" in the overall publications program.

A number of years ago a small informal committee reviewing publications at MIT suggested the establishment of a publications council:

> That a Publications Council be established to conduct a review of the concept and plan for publications of administrative activities, delegating daily operations to the Office of Publications and Public Relations as it sees fit; to conduct a continuing broad review of the Institute's total publications activity; and to coordinate this activity with the academic, development, alumni, and public relations programs.
>
> The Publications Council might be made up of the Vice President, Academic Affairs, the Vice President for Development, the Dean of Student Affairs, a representative of the Faculty, the Director of Public Relations, and the Director of Publications; it should occasionally meet with other officers, such as the Director of Admissions, for consideration of their publications needs. It should consult from time to time with experts in various areas, such as faculty members who are authorities on design and communications and publications specialists from outside the Institute.
>
> It should meet at least once a year with the President to review past publications and plans for future ones. His judgment as to the tone of Institute publications, their purposes and budgetary allocations is essential.

Many of the questions suggested as proper topics for a publications committee are questions that the director of the publications office ought to be asking throughout the year. A director who is buried under a day-to-day avalanche of detail may be unable to stand back and take a detached and analytical view of the operation. If a good advisory committee is not on hand for this purpose, the publications director needs to hold frequent staff meetings and occasionally schedule special retreats. Equally valuable are professional meetings where the director can see how the institution's program stacks up against those of other colleges and universities.

Is more money the answer?

It's easy to believe that any publications program could be improved by more money and more (or better) staff. However, the administration's response to requests for more is almost always, "What can you do to improve your program and still live within your budget?" The only honest answer may well be, "If you want a better program, you're going to have to spend more money."

On the other hand, although we can all use more money, it's not always the answer. Some institutions are asked to produce too much for too little money. But for most, it is a question of how the money is used, not how much is used. Here are seven ideas that may help you produce quality publications on a limited budget:

1. *Who* controls the budget is more important than the size of the budget.
2. Cutting just eight pages of excess copy from a catalog may pay for a week

of shooting by a top-flight photographer.

3. A small, good booklet is better than a run-of-the-mill large one. If you must cut, cut your copy and trim down your mailing lists.

4. You *can* find good graphic designers. Some of the country's leading commercial designers have done college brochures at cut rates. Give them plenty of time and room to swing creatively.

5. Well-written copy is the heart of all good publications and offers an inexpensive way to demonstrate the intellectual quality of your institution.

6. Good taste is not expensive, but poor taste cannot be covered up by high-priced printing.

7. Simplicity in copy, illustration, and design can improve the effectiveness of your publications—and save you money.

Keep good records for better budgets

Living within a fixed budget is never easy, but only governments can get away with deficit financing for very long. The publications manager who runs in the red too many years in a row won't have much job security.

One of the keys to living within a budget is having a hand in shaping it. No publications office can do an adequate job today if it must live within last year's budget or that of the year before.

Accurate cost records are essential to the planning of meaningful budgets. You should keep up-to-date information on every publication processed during the year. As soon as a job comes in the door, it should be logged into the office computer. Each step of production can then be quickly recorded as it occurs. You can access computer records to develop analytical studies of costs, production schedules, and budget activity.

The file should contain the following information on each printing job:

• all production specifications including quantity, size, paper, ink, type, and binding;

• estimated printing cost; and

• total costs, including composition, printing, design, photography, and mailing charges.

You should also have a system for recording consecutively numbered printing requisitions and purchase order numbers together with the production dates for each publication. A handy way to keep track of jobs is to have a printed file folder on which all specifications are entered. This folder can also hold papers and correspondence about the job as well as a finished copy of the publication.

Knowing what has been done gives you a good start in preparing next year's budget since many jobs are repeated from year to year. However, you must also have an idea of where you want to go and the impact of changing graphic arts technology on your future plans. For instance, it has only been in the last 15 or 20 years that web offset has been a practical printing process for use in college work. The quality of web offset work has improved greatly, and it is now an economical process in runs of fewer than 20,000. It also opens up possibilities for four-color process work that were never before within the budget range of most institutions.

The graphic arts industry is a rapidly changing field, and if we are to get the most for our publications dollar, we need to be aware of its technological developments and learn how best to take advantage of them.

Evaluation and analysis

Once you have organized an office, acquired a competent staff, and are living within your budget, how do you know what kind of job your publications are really doing? Evaluation and analysis are two of the most difficult functions of publications management. You can get an idea of the graphic attractiveness of your publications by calling on consultants for their advice or by entering your pieces in competition with the work of other institutions. But how do you find out if your magazine is really being read or if your catalogs provide the type of information that prospective students need?

The usual testing methods employed by the communications industry are not practical for colleges and universities because of the high costs of surveying low-circulation publications. A thorough readership study would cost more than the piece itself. Letters to the editor are certainly no valid gauge of editorial competence. Return coupons do no more than measure the advertising effectiveness of a direct mail brochure. Mass testing techniques are not valid because you are not trying to communicate with a mass audience, but rather with a variety of specialized audiences. You can do low-cost readership studies, but you must take care to follow recommended procedures as to structuring the questionnaire, drawing a random sample, ensuring an adequate return, and analyzing the data.

One thing you can do is to make sure you *are* communicating with those groups that you must reach. Start by making a list of every piece produced for your institution annually. This list should include the title, a general description of the publication, the date it was published, quantity, cost, and its major and secondary audiences. By then separating the publications into audience groupings such as alumni, prospective students, development prospects, students, and faculty, you can quickly see which pieces overlap and which communications areas are not being adequately covered.

You may also find that while you're not speaking at all to some of the institution's important publics, others are being deluged with materials.

For example, you should screen the mass of printed material sent to high school counselors. An evaluation technique used successfully by a number of institutions is the college-day visit. You invite a small and carefully selected group of high school counselors and teachers to campus to learn more about the institution and to give their views on printed materials they are receiving. Informal get-togethers with high school students have also been helpful, but perhaps of more value are reviews of catalog content and recruiting material with freshmen soon after they have arrived on campus.

In the end, the publications manager has to develop the skills, the taste, and the sensitivity to measure the product of the office against others and to judge it objectively. Good publications management means not only recognizing when you have a successful program, but knowing how to employ the necessary techniques to create one.

Chapter 3

Editing and Writing Techniques

An editor edits. He or she prepares the work of others for publication. The editor employs certain skills that are distinct from the creative skills of the writer. Only rarely does one person possess the talents of both a first-rate writer and a first-rate editor.

This book does not purport to be a basic course in editing. To learn the fundamentals of editing—which apply to editors of college publications as well as to those who edit newspapers, magazines, and books—you can study a number of excellent texts. The bibliography in this book includes several that cover this area of copy preparation.

We do, however, wish to examine some of the specific applications of editing in the college publications field, to share some experiences, to suggest some policies, and to warn against some pitfalls. For the academic situation presents certain challenges and hazards to college and university editors that those in the commercial world may never encounter.

Who writes the copy?

First of all, a college publications office that attempts to assume not only the editing but the writing function for all or most of the publications it processes will probably find itself hopelessly understaffed. The typical college or university publications office keeps its staff busy editing, illustrating, proofreading, getting printing bids or writing specifications, seeing publications through the press, and distributing publications.

In order to keep the flow of publications moving, the publications office has to rely on other campus offices to generate most of the copy. For example, the registrar compiles the catalog, the dean of students prepares the student handbook, and others assemble the class schedule, the directory, and the financial report. Many of the officials who prepare these materials would be reluctant to give up this responsibility, and there is no reason they should.

The editor's role is to review the material, reorganize it if necessary, improve the readability, make it conform to style, cut out unnecessary words and phrases, and prepare it for the printer. The editor should establish rules on how copy should be prepared. No editor should accept or send to the typesetter handwritten or single-spaced copy or copy with more than a very few changes written in. All copy should be ready for editing when it comes to the editor's office. It should be double-spaced on one side of a sheet. Insertions should be clearly identified as "Copy A," "Copy B," and so on. Little slips of paper stuck to the original or submitted in loose form will likely be lost.

The publications office may also research and write copy for some publications. For example, the faculty/staff newsletter may originate in the editor's office, as may the viewbook, the faculty handbook, and various brochures.

We don't want to suggest that the publications office should not generate copy for some publications. The pedestrian standards of writing in many college publications reveal a weak link in the communications process. Publications offices seem to have more success persuading top administrators to hire editors and graphic designers than writers, and few offices employ staff members whose sole or primary responsibility is to write effective copy. As a result, graphic standards have risen dramatically during the past 30 years while the copy often remains stodgy, legalistic, and dull, dull, dull.

One solution might be to hire free-lance writers for important publications such as the basic admissions piece or the student handbook. These writers could start from scratch and do the research and interviewing that go into any good piece of informational writing. They could take the time to do the rewriting that produces a polished piece of prose.

Above all, the writer can pay more attention to the nature of the reading public for a specific publication. Some publications go to high school juniors and others to alumni of the class of 1940. Some try to persuade college graduates to enroll in a Ph.D. program, and others try to interest disadvantaged students in taking a remedial English course before tackling a full college load. Rarely do manuscripts from deans and department heads reveal any tailoring to specific readers.

Genial editors must not allow themselves to accept responsibilities that are not theirs. If they do, their other publications will suffer. And they will soon become known as an easy touch—especially to those on campus who are always all too ready to "pass the buck to the editor." Editors should enforce a strict policy regarding the writing of materials or they may find themselves swamped with these chores, while the essential job of editing regular publications is postponed or neglected. They may simply refuse to accept the writing responsibility for any but certain specified publications for which they have been given full responsibility. And they should insist that anyone asking for writing assistance come prepared with the necessary facts and research and preferably with a rough draft.

In other words, unless they have unusual talents and energy or huge staffs, college editors must insist that colleagues on the faculty and in other offices do their part in bringing ideas to the stage of finished printed pieces. Editors can work with these colleagues, but they probably cannot agree to assume the full responsibility for more than a handful of the institution's publications without slighting other publications.

The editor's authority

Editors must have a clear understanding of the limits of their authority. If they are held responsible for all publications bearing the college or university imprint, they cannot afford to approve copy they or their designated assistants have not personally reviewed.

Many people will ask editors to give their copy a "once over lightly." They will plead that they are behind schedule, that the publication should have been delivered a week ago, that it is a routine job. These people may not want to submit their copy to the editor's authority, but they do want some assurance that someone in authority has looked at the material in case they run into trouble later on. Editors who allow themselves to be trapped into these informal arrangements may regret it. Should a serious error or libelous statement slip by, the writer may truthfully say, "The editor looked at it and gave us an OK." The fact that the writer pressured the editor into bypassing the regular careful procedures is easily forgotten by everyone but the unfortunate editor.

It's better to have a firm policy to assume all of the responsibility for a publication or none. Maintaining a halfway position is as difficult as being half pregnant.

We also recommend that editors refuse to provide spur-of-the-moment cost estimates unless they are sure that the estimate will be within 10 percent of the final cost. Perhaps an editor remembers an identical job done in the past few months and can easily check the records. Otherwise the customer must provide full specifications for the project and allow the editor at least 48 hours in which to prepare the estimate or obtain a bid. More than likely the publication in question has been in the works for weeks or months, and a short delay to obtain an accurate cost estimate will not sabotage the project.

An editor who yields to pleas to give off-the-cuff estimates may be horrified to discover these guesses incorporated in the minutes of committee meetings and forming the basis of bitter debates at faculty meetings. Professional printing estimators take their time to do a thorough job of estimating, and there is no reason why a college editor should be expected to provide curb service for colleagues.

Resisting change for the sake of change

The publications office needs a policy on changes in text, pictures, and format. You cannot maintain a stable of publications, whether a dozen or 500, and successfully undertake a complete remodeling job on each one every year. That is, you cannot if you have a normal staff and printing appropriations.

Some people demand novelty every year. If the catalog has had the same cover for two years with only minor changes, they moan that they have been looking at the same cover for decades.

Superior admissions booklets, catalogs, faculty handbooks, and the like do not happen by chance or overnight. Months and even years of planning go into their execution. Reader reaction provides clues to changes after the initial printing. Comments by prospective and enrolled students, faculty members, alumni, and other publics can refine the formula to produce a more useful and readable publication. But the editor should not be asked to come up with a completely different design every year.

The catalog, for example, is a publication that must be kept as up-to-date as possible, even though some of its information is obsolete before it arrives from the printer's. A complete redesign should probably not be undertaken more than every five or six years. Changing the date and the color of the cover should be enough to distinguish one edition from the next, and every few years you can introduce a new cover design. A thorough reexamination of the catalog according to its main objectives, organization, format, and readability may involve dozens of people over a period of a year or two.

Part of the temptation in the "change for change's sake" attitude is that editors and college personnel get tired of seeing the same cover or format on the catalog and other regular publications. But you should remember that the catalog is probably a brand-new publication for prospective students and other off-campus audiences. And current students are likely to value the continuity of seeing the same cover on such publications as the catalog and student handbook.

Readability

Both writers and editors can benefit by dipping into Strunk and White, Gunning, or Zinsser. All of these stylists emphasize the basic rules of readability: active voice, strong verbs, short sentences, familiar words, personal references, and variety of constructions.

Of some value to college editors are the various readability tests of which the Flesch test and the Robert Gunning Fog Index are the best known. These tests seek to determine the level of education a reader must have to understand a piece of writing. You can use the readability criteria to broaden the reader base. By emphasizing shorter words and sentences and personal references and by avoiding obscure and exotic words, you can bring your copy within the reading ability of its intended audience.

Here's how the Gunning Fog Index works: Calculate the average sentence length for a sample of 10 sentences in the piece you want to test. Then count the number of words of more than two syllables in a 100-word sample, but don't count the following:

- capitalized words;

- three-syllable words formed by adding "es" or "ed" to verb forms; and
- words that are combinations of two words such as "bookkeeper."

Add the average sentence length and the number of words with more than two syllables and multiply this number by 0.4. The answer represents the number of years of education a reader needs to understand the piece of writing. For example, a score of 13 indicates that the piece has a reading level appropriate to someone who has completed a year of college.

More and more editors are processing copy on a computer and can take advantage of such software as Grammatik, RightWriter, Correct Grammar, and Readability Plus. These programs and others can spot mistakes in grammar, measure readability, flag obsolete and colloquial terms, highlight frequent use of the passive voice, and the like, but no one program does everything.

Applying readability formulas to a college catalog will in almost all cases produce a rating that goes off the chart. For example, a catalog may include course descriptions such as the following:

> Physics 560. Introduction to Wave Mechanics. Origins, de Broglie's hypothesis, uncertainty principle. Solutions of Schrodinger's equation. Properties of angular momentum. Matrices and applications in quantum mechanics. Perturbation theory, scattering problems, interaction with electromagnetic radiation.

There is little or nothing you can do about descriptions like this. You can't rewrite the physics curriculum so that French or history majors can understand it. (Chances are you don't understand it yourself.) All you can do is make sure everything is spelled correctly and devote your editing skills to the general portions of the catalog.

While readability formulas can be helpful, don't apply them too rigidly. They are no substitute for the brain teasing and sweat that go into a first-rate job of organization and writing. It's not necessary to abandon forever the three-syllable word or the complicated sentence. Too many short sentences composed of short words create choppy, dull writing.

Misguided communications specialists have sometimes adopted the doubtful thesis that, since short words and short sentences and paragraphs improve readability, the general reader will never read more than a few hundred words about anything. They give every piece of copy the same diagnosis and prescription— "too long, cut it down." This formula and a few others serve as substitutes for careful copy analysis.

People will read about subjects that interest them or that they must know— regardless of the number of words used. Someone who lacks motivation may not read 50 words, but the person who is motivated may feel cheated at getting only 10,000. Consider some of the all-time best-sellers—*Gone with the Wind, The Rise and Fall of the Third Reich,* and *Roots,* for example. These are not short books, but they were bought *and* read.

Take your own case at this moment, dear reader. If you are reading this book because you are involved with college or university publications, you are probably willing to overlook the verbosity and any deficiencies in style of the authors of these pages in order to gain a few ideas to help you in your job.

The "short-copy formula" would be appropriate only if you were interested in the quick hard sell. Direct mail specialists know they must get their message across with a gimmick and a few words. Usually what they have to sell interests only a tiny fraction of the people who will receive their mailings.

People who have no interest in your institution and its problems and programs will not develop an interest by reading your 100-word letter. In fact, they probably won't even bother to read it. But those people who already have an interest— parents, alumni, students, taxpayers, staff members, townspeople, trustees, or contributors—may be willing and eager to read what you have to say even though it takes 5,000 well-chosen words to say it.

The "keep it short" school offers no real editorial formula for the serious college communicator. What sells magazine subscriptions and neckties may not sell higher education.

Using a style guide

The publications office also needs to decide whether to use a style guide or manual and, if so, which one. Every newspaper, magazine, and book publisher sets a style to ensure some degree of uniformity. The editor will, of course, follow the ordinary rules of grammar and abide by a good dictionary, but decisions of style are necessarily arbitrary. In preparing a style book, the editor is making a personal judgment. He or she can make many choices: Will you use a comma before "and" in a series? Will you write out numbers up to nine and then use numerals? Will you use U.S. Postal Service two-letter abbreviations for states?

Without adhering to any style, a publications office with more than one editorial worker will be unable to maintain any consistency. Thus a single booklet may refer to a professor as Dr. John Jones; Mr. John Jones; John Jones; Jones; J. Jones; Assistant Dean John Jones; John Jones, Ph.D.; Professor John Jones; and so on. Some institutions solve this problem by decreeing that all faculty and staff members be referred to in official publications by the highest rank that the college confers. Any member of the instructional staff above instructor would be referred to as "Professor," not "Dr." or "Mr."

Style must be arbitrary, but it should make sense, and it should be flexible. The new college president may prefer to have his or her name written in a particular way; the college may wish to avoid certain expressions that do not have official sanction; students may call the science building "Barnum Hall" when its name was changed 30 years ago to "Science and Technology." By incorporating these local decisions in the style book, the editor can, in a small way, promote the objectives of the institution.

In fact, any editor who has been on the job more than a week knows that it is far more of a headache to try to play by ear without a style than it is to follow set rules. Playing by ear soon leads to inconsistencies that can be used as evidence by anyone with a preference for one style or another.

Some editorial offices prepare their own style manuals, while others adopt the *Associated Press Stylebook,* the Government Printing Office style manual, or the *Chicago Manual of Style.* A publications office may use AP style for its periodicals and the *Chicago Manual* for its other publications. See the Appendix for a sample of one university's style book. (In this book—except for the Appendix—we have followed CASE style, which is based in part on the *AP Stylebook* and in part on the *Chicago Manual of Style.* CASE also uses *Webster's New World Dictionary, Third College Edition.*)

Proofreading: It's never enough!

Despite careful proofreading, errors do creep into publications. They usually become most apparent immediately after delivery of the first copy. One technique you can use to cut down on the number of errors is to read through every job one last time before giving it an OK to print. Long before this, you should have read galleys and pages and perhaps received a set of revised proofs; and, you hope, the customer has also given the publication additional proofreadings.

Nevertheless, just before releasing the job to the printer, you might ask someone who has never seen the copy to read it through for sense. This procedure often turns up typographical errors that have slipped through the proofreading net. It costs something to provide this extra reading, and it may delay the job by hours or even days, but nothing hurts the reputation of an editorial office more than frequent typos. Not every layperson can spot good writing or good layout or good artwork, but many people can catch a typo, and readers always enjoy finding mistakes that the experts have missed.

Photographs: No substitute for words

The idea that "one picture is worth a thousand words" has received a wider hearing than it deserves. Today anyone who questions the value of good photography in college publications is 50 years behind the times. But we would still insist that photography is an editorial tool to be used to accomplish the job for which it was intended. It will not work miracles. Photographs will not do what only words can do.

Those editors who overemphasize the role of photographs probably do it for one of two reasons: Either they really believe that good photography can replace good writing, or they don't have the time—or the ability—to prepare readable, well-organized copy. They run some nice photos and hope to "say it with pictures."

Photographs have an important place in college and university publications, but you cannot use a photograph to explain registration procedures, admissions requirements, housing regulations, and so on. It would save a lot of time and effort if a classy photo *could* replace the hours and even days an editor might spend developing and then polishing a clear and readable description of admission policies that leaves no room for ambiguity or misunderstanding. Unfortunately, in the real world, most of the time you'll have to say it with words.

You might say in some instances that "one *good* picture is worth a thousand words." But many pictures are not worth five words, much less a thousand. They do not tell a story, show any creativity, or even demonstrate a minimum technical acceptability.

The need for good writing

Much of the criticism directed against college publications is justified. Francis C. Pray, a respected fund-raising consultant, once wrote:

> It has gradually been borne upon me over the years that only occasionally do I see one of these beautifully printed, handsomely illustrated typographical gems that ever really says anything—that contains any writing of quality to maintain interest after the appearance of the book has won for it the first look. I have begun to realize that the average slick college brochure is atrociously written, has little of interest to commend it, is not aimed at a particular group, and is a wasteful, expensive communications medium. The average "beautiful" brochure is like a rosewood inlaid box filled with sand.

If you fear these comments may apply to your own writing, take heart. Remember, even sand can be made into a windowpane, a television tube, or even the lens of a telescope. So shoot for the stars; edit and polish your words until they become meaningful—and readable—communication.

How do you do this? If you're a beginner, you can learn from others. Don't be ashamed to borrow the good idea of a colleague in another institution, provided you give credit when appropriate and provided you offer a few new ideas yourself as your skill and expertise develop. You can also collect representative samples of publications from other institutions, study the winners in CASE's Recognition Program, attend seminars and lectures on good writing, and read good literature in other fields. And, always, you should be practicing your craft.

Finally, you should try to establish confidence in your ability as an editor. Too many cooks, too many censors will spoil the publication. You need to have the final word on all projects for which you have the final responsibility. Good publications are not produced by committees. You were hired to edit publications, and presumably this means you have the training and competence to do the job well. You cannot conduct a responsible publications program if you don't have the authority that goes with the title.

Chapter 4

Buying Composition And Printing

I t is unwise to pay too much, but worse to pay too little. When you pay too much, you lose a little money. That is all. But when you pay too little, you sometimes lose all, because the thing you bought was incapable of doing the thing it was bought to do. The common law of business balance prohibits paying *little* and getting a *lot*. It can't be done. If you deal with the lowest bidder, it is well to add something for the risk you run. And if you do that you will have enough to pay for something better (John Ruskin).

Someone once compared buying a printing job to buying a tailor-made suit: You can get it cheaper by cutting corners on workmanship, materials, or style, but a low price is no bargain if the suit doesn't fit. What purchasing agent would buy a size 34 suit at any price if his fit is a size 42? Who would ask the tailor, "How much would the suit be if you leave out the pockets?" Yet these are exactly the kind of suggestions made in all seriousness by well-meaning and economy-oriented college administrators and business officers.

Since no two printing jobs are exactly alike, you cannot buy good printing the same way you would buy paper towels, office supplies, or sweatshirts for the football team.

Cost is not the only criterion

Another title for this chapter might be "How *Not* to Buy Printing." One way *not* to buy printing is on the basis of cost alone. In printing, as in anything else, you generally get what you pay for. Benjamin Franklin, who in his time was both a printer and a buyer of printing, said good printing was an investment but poor printing was an expense.

Unfortunately, many public colleges and universities are forced to put out all of their printing on a low-price public bid basis. The only way in which they can achieve anything approaching fine quality printing is to write such detailed and carefully worded specifications that only certain printers can qualify for the bidding. Unfortunately, many college publications offices must resort to this practice in order to produce effective work.

There is always the danger that a printer who has been awarded a contract for printing at an extremely marginal price may be tempted to cut corners on the job in order to make a normal profit. A printer can do this in many ways. A job that is in the printing plant on a strictly marginal basis will not receive the same attention as a job on which the printer is making at least a small profit. There might be a temptation to substitute a cheaper grade of paper or to deliver a short count, although this is something that the alert printing buyer should be able to spot.

Anyone buying printing should be familiar with Printing Trade Customs adopted by the Graphic Arts Council of North America. A trade custom has been defined as "any practice or method of doing business which is done so regularly in a particular industry as to justify an expectation by the parties that it will be observed with respect to a questioned transaction."

For example, trade customs allow a printer to review a bid that has not been accepted 60 days after submission. If a particular publication is delayed beyond this period, you are expected to give the printer an opportunity to adjust the bid. A substantial increase in paper costs might also call for a review of the bid.

Again, if you provide color separations for a job, these separations belong to your institution. But even if you ask the printer to order the separations, you can add a statement to your bid to the effect that you retain ownership of the separations. A printer who does not wish to go along with this request need not bid.

Probably the trade custom that creates the most problems for clients is the one covering overs and unders: "Overrun or underruns not to exceed 10 percent on quantities ordered, or the percentages agreed upon, shall constitute acceptable delivery." In other words, in the absence of any other agreement, a printer can deliver 10 percent over the quantity ordered or 10 percent under this quantity. The printer adjusts the bill accordingly. Sometimes clients who order, say, 10,000 copies of a booklet may balk at paying for 10,500. The publications specialist should explain this trade custom before the bids are sent out.

You can specify an exception in your bid. Let's say you want to send a mailing to 50,000 alumni. You can't get by with only 45,000 copies, and you have no use for 5,000 extra copies. You can write your bid to specify no underrun and no more than, say, 5 percent overrun. This departure from trade customs means that most printers will have to add something to their bid if anything goes wrong and they end up with 48,000 copies and have to go back on press. But you will get as many as you need for your mailing.

The general rule is that if you want an exception to the trade customs, you must work this out with the printer before the purchase order is written and accepted.

Getting bids

While there is a danger in submitting all of your printing to open low bidding, there is also a danger in buying your printing without any competition among printers.

If you have a job that you feel a number of printers can do equally well, the best printing-buying procedure is selective bidding—that is, you ask for bids from three or four printers you believe are fully qualified to do a good job on that particular piece. Always try to get at least three bids for major jobs such as catalogs, annual reports, development brochures, alumni magazines, and so on.

Writing clear and precise specifications is a key element in obtaining good printing quotations. Leave nothing out, nothing to chance. The result will improve business relations with your printer, make your job easier, speed publication delivery, and stretch your printing budget. (See the sample printing and composition bid forms on the next pages.) Knowing exactly what you want before you meet with a printer or ask for bids calls for advance planning and budgeting. Meeting with busy deans and vice presidents and persuading them to approve future budget commitments can be the toughest part of your work in preparing accurate publication specifications.

For small jobs, it is impractical to ask for formal bids. An informal price query over the telephone to the printer is usually sufficient. More time and effort would be wasted in attempting to get formal bids for small jobs than can ever be saved.

It's a good idea to have a rough cost estimate of your printing job before you ask for bids. Every publications office should keep a file of all previous jobs. This means if you have done a similar job before, you should have records of how much it cost. You'll probably have to pay more today for labor, paper, and so on, but at least you will have a ballpark figure in your mind before getting a final estimate. (In the last 10 years, labor and materials costs for printing have risen on the average of 5 to 7 percent annually.) Keep necessary information—job number, press run, date, vendor, and the like—in your computer or on 3 by 5 cards. Then, even on infrequently printed jobs that come up only every two or three years, you can find a helpful starting point in your file.

Contracts for long-term publications

You might consider a two- or three-year contract for bulletins or other long-term major publications such as your alumni magazine or university quarterly. A two- or three-year printing contract provides stability of price and budget planning as well as the savings that can be made by the long-term purchase of paper. You might also get a special price because your printer knows that this work would be in the shop for two or three years. There might also be savings on offset negatives (which could be held and reused from one year to the next), standardized paper sizes, and the benefit of the printer's experience with the job.

The sample contract specification form on pages 32-33 is used by a large university in contracting for the printing of its catalogs.

Office of Publications

printing bid

Purdue University
Building D, South Campus Courts
West Lafayette, Indiana 47907
(317) 494-2034

Date _____

Title of Publication _____

_____

Quantity _____ Size _____ Number of pages _____

Binding _____

Stock: Text _____

       Cover _____

Inks: Text _____

       Cover _____

Types _____

Halftones _____

Proofs _____

Quotation Due _____ Copy to Printer _____ Delivery Date _____

Additional Instructions

Bid _____

       F.O.B. West Lafayette, Indiana

_____   _____

(signed)   Date

OFFICE OF PUBLICATIONS COPY

Office of Publications

Purdue University
Building D, South Campus Courts
West Lafayette, Indiana 47907
(317) 494-2034

composition bid

Date _____

Job title _____

TEXT: _____

character	size and face	measure
_____	_____	_____
_____	_____	_____
_____	_____	_____

Other specifications _____

_____

_____

HEADS: _____

Number	size and face
_____	_____
_____	_____
_____	_____

Other specifications _____

_____

_____

Kinds of proofs desired: Galley _____ Page _____ Reproduction _____

Proofs delivered within _____ working days   Bid wanted by _____

Bid _____   _____
F.O.B. West Lafayette, Indiana   (signed)

OFFICE OF PUBLICATIONS COPY

31

SECTION I
Scope of Printing

Printing covered by this contract shall be offset printing of catalogs made up of continuous reading matter and illustrations and printed on book, coated and/or cover paper, including the binding of such printed matter as specified, the tipping or folding in of inserts, and the finishing of such printed matter complete as ordered.

SECTION II
General Conditions

1. *Period of Contract.* A contract placed under these specifications shall be in effect for a period starting with September 1, 19____, and terminating August 31, 19____.

2. *Breaching of Contract.* In the event a contractor fails to perform work under his contract, or breaches provisions thereof, the University shall notify the contractor in writing of the contractor's failure, and if after five days from the mailing of such notice the failure is not remedied, the University may order printing from a source competent to do the work and any loss sustained by the University in thus changing printers shall be considered as a justifiable claim against the contractor.

3. *Subcontracting.* No contractor may subcontract or sublet any portion of printing in the performance of this contract without written consent obtained in advance from the Publications Office of the University.

4. *Renewal of Contract.* A printing contract may be renewed for a period of one year provided the University gives the contractor 60 days written notice of its desire to do so and contractor accepts such continuation in writing 30 or more days before the expiration of the contract.

5. *Jobs Incapable of Production under these Specifications.* If manuscripts or copy is sent to the contractor to be printed under the specifications herein for ordinary composition and presswork, and the contractor believes that such manuscript or copy cannot be fairly composed or printed under these specifications, he shall immediately notify the University before beginning the work, and shall state in writing what he believes is a fair basis for the work.

6. *Placing of Orders.* All printing shall be done on written order from the Purchasing Division of the University and in accordance with the terms and conditions of the contract.

7. *Acknowledgment of Order, Copy, and Proof.* The contractor shall acknowledge an order and the manuscript or copy and proof pertaining to the same in the manner and at the time prescribed by the University.

8. *Acceptance of Delivery Date.* The acceptance by the contractor of an order containing a delivery date is evidence of his belief that the delivery date as set in the order is reasonable, and of his agreement to meet the delivery date.

9. *Overtime.* No overtime shall be charged without permission from the Publications Office of the University. Increased costs due to overtime shall take into

consideration only the increases due to labor.

10. *Quality of Work and Determination Thereof.* All work done and all material used under these specifications shall be of good quality, and the accepted trade customs and definitions of the printing industry shall determine the attainment of that ideal.

11. *Proofs.* Proofs shall be submitted as specified on each order and a place shall be provided thereon for approval and the date of approval. Proofs shall be sent to the Publications Office of the University as directed.

12. *Preservation of Manuscript and Proof.* The contractor shall hold all proof and manuscript for a period of 60 days after the delivery of a completed article, or, if the contractor has not billed the University within that time, for a period of two weeks after the delivery of the bill; and the University shall have the right to ask for the proofs or manuscript for inspection at any time within that period.

13. *Costs of Packing and Deliveries.* All costs of cartons, wrapping, and shipping materials, and of transportation and delivery to the proper officer of the University shall be borne by the contractor.

14. *Methods of Packing.* All material produced under these specifications should be packed in bundles of 50, 100, or 200, as may be specified on separate orders. On each carton shall be pasted a label or stenciled information containing the address of the University, the title of the bulletin, the University order number, and number of copies the carton contains. For certain printing, the University may specify that certain additional information be placed on the label. Each order shall be packed in separate cartons weighing no more than 60 pounds filled.

15. *Billing.* The contractor shall submit bills in triplicate and refer to the purchase order number. Each bill shall give a detailed breakdown of costs for each publication.

16. *Payments.* The University will make payment for all work coming under these specifications within 30 days after the rendering of the invoice and the delivery of the printing, provided the work is acceptable and the printing and work incident thereto have been done in accordance with the specifications.

17. *Contingencies.* The contractor shall not be held responsible for any loss, damage, or delay in furnishing any printing covered by these specifications caused by fires, strikes, civil or military authorities, acts of God or of a public enemy, or other causes beyond his control.

How much should it cost?

There are few standard factors in computing the cost of printing jobs because no two printing jobs are exactly alike. In one case, the type may cost more because you are faced with unusual author's alterations. Another may be a rush job or one you want the printer to do as fill-in work.

Even the time of the year may affect the cost. A job done when the shop is full, perhaps when it is turning out Christmas catalogs or has a heavy load of commercial work, is apt to cost you more than if it were printed in a slack season. The printer's overhead is constant and wages are fairly constant; nevertheless, it is common practice to trim prices in order to get work into the shop during a slack season. With experience, you should be able to estimate within 15 to 20 percent of what a job will cost, but don't expect to come up with an exact figure; the variable factors are too great.

The basic factors: Cost, service, quality

When you are buying printing, you will consider three basic factors: cost, service, and quality. Most printing is bought on the strength of one or two of these three points. It depends upon the nature of the publication which of the three is most important. Rarely would all three be equally important in one job.

If you are producing an annual report—a showpiece for the institution—you should buy the best printing you can afford. And if you know that you won't get the final copy of the president's message until three weeks before the scheduled delivery date, then the second factor, service or speed, will also be important. You would probably tell the printer to do anything, including working nights and Sundays, in order to get the job out. For this service, you would expect to pay and pay plenty. That eliminates the first factor, cost, from this particular job.

On the other hand, if you are producing a quarterly of student English themes for which there is a modest budget and for which you have ample time to plan and edit, your most important factor in buying printing would be low cost. You would try to find a printer who would do a reasonably good job and maybe even give you a special price in exchange for being able to use the job as a fill-in whenever the workload at the plant was slack. A printer must pay strippers and pressmen whether they are working or not and often is happy to get jobs that will just carry the overhead.

Selecting a printer

The most important step in buying printing is the selection of the printer. First of all, as in buying anything, you should look at samples. Most printers will be eager to display their most glamorous brochures, and you may find yourself looking at a desk full of four-color jobs when almost all of your work is in one or two colors. You can't blame printing salespeople for wanting to show you the best jobs that have gone through their shop, but you should insist on seeing pieces that are similar to your project. Once you have reviewed 10 to 12 printing samples, you can make some judgment on the general quality and tone of the printer's work.

When visiting a new restaurant, connoisseurs of fine food will often ask to see the kitchen before ordering a meal. When you are considering a new printer, it's a good idea to visit the printer's plant. While a clean, well-lighted, and efficiently laid-out pressroom does not guarantee good printing, sloppy housekeeping, heaps of scrap paper on the floor, and dirty presses seldom add up to top-notch work.

There is usually some correlation between the care a printer takes of the plant and equipment and the care the firm will give your job. Looking at the work on the presses will give you some idea of the kind and quality of work the printer normally runs.

The size and location of the printer's plant are also important. Many jobs can be done at a distance, but if your publication requires constant supervision and editorial changes, you may find it more convenient, even if the initial cost is slightly more, to choose a printer close at hand.

Also consider the size of the printing plant. If you are producing half a dozen small publications a year, it wouldn't make sense to buy your printing from a giant magazine plant or publication printer. If the printer does accept your work (and he or she may not), your small job may get lost among the many long-run production jobs being put through the plant. On the other hand, if the plant is too small (just one press and limited typesetting facilities), it would be hard-pressed to give you the service and the speed that a larger shop could offer.

In general, there are two kinds of printers: those few who can be called "creative printers" and those who belong to the great majority of commercial shops.

A creative printer not only reproduces your publication mechanically, but can supply creative design help and, in many instances, artwork. A number of printing companies across the country specialize in college and university publications. These printers will design a publication from beginning to end, specifying type, paper, and ink and even supplying copy, photos, and art if need be. This type of service is valuable for the small college or school that does not have a large enough publications program to hire its own staff.

The bulk of the printers with whom we must deal are commercial, not creative printers. While they may do an adequate layout or typographical job, usually their work is unimaginative. They are best at taking the design you supply and putting out a faithful reproduction.

If you can find a good designer either on your faculty or in the community, use him or her. It is often less expensive than paying the printer for this service, and your final product will probably show more originality and better represent your institution. If possible, design the publication, with professional help, in your own shop, and wrap it up as completely as possible before turning it over to a trade printer.

Some few college or university publications offices buy not only printing but all of the separate elements such as typesetting, color separations, presswork, paper, and binding that make up the finished job. To act as your own printing "broker" requires long experience in printing methods and production. For any but the most expert, this practice of buying the parts of a job is not only time-consuming but can even be very costly.

Choosing and buying the paper

It is also impractical for most colleges to buy and store the paper necessary for catalogs and other publications. Although most printers charge you a markup of 10 to 40 percent over what they paid for the paper they use to print your job, this is not as outrageous as it may appear. For a short-run job using expensive paper, the waste could easily run to 30 percent of the paper.

In general, it does not pay to buy your own paper unless you are using at least a carload of one kind of paper in a year's time. Even then you have problems of insurance, storage, moisture control, aging, and trucking the paper to the printer.

Don't be afraid to learn something about paper. You don't need to become a paper expert, but learn enough so that you can specify proper weights and finishes as well as colors. Paper plays an important part in the design of all publications. There are many fascinating textures, shades, and colors of cover and text paper. You can get paper with a different color on each side; you can use a paper with an unusual texture as part of your design.

Most paper is sold by weight. For this reason, you shouldn't specify a paper that is heavier than you need. For example, there is a 20 percent difference in price between a 50-pound paper and a 60-pound paper. In a catalog, where paper constitutes from 25 to 50 percent of the cost of the total job, using 50-pound instead of 60-pound paper in an order of 20,000 to 30,000 catalogs could save you more than several hundred dollars.

A number of universities with long-run catalogs are now using ground wood stock or newsprint for the text portions of these publications. Newsprint can save money but should not be used for any publication expected to last more than a year as it yellows and becomes brittle after that time.

Most paper companies will be eager to supply you with sample books, which are invaluable aids to planning and designing publications. The samples in these paper books are single sheets or small swatches.

If you want to see the actual size, feel, and weight of a publication before it is printed, your printer or paper supplier will make up a complete dummy. This can be an important step in planning any major publication. Before you select the paper for your annual report or development brochure, have the printer make up two or three dummies using different inside stocks and covers. Ask the printer to tell you which papers of those you have selected will run best in the presses and will take the best impression.

Only two raw materials go into any printing job: paper and ink. How they are used depends on the skill of the designer and of the printer, and it's up to you to select the best paper—and the best printer—for the job.

Using color

Although you can improve many printing jobs by introducing a second color, you may wish to stay away from three-color printing jobs. Three-color printing necessitates either running the publication twice on a two-color press or using a four-color press, which will cost more money and will not generally be much more effective than a two-color piece.

More and more colleges are turning to full color for many of their student recruitment and fund-raising publications. The evolution from black and white or two-color to full-color publications should surprise no one. Outside of old movies (and some of these have been colorized), how much black and white TV is still around? Readers have become accustomed to color in the major daily newspapers and magazines. A black and white viewbook, no matter how great the photos and design, may stay on the giveaway table in the high school gym while the more colorful booklets are taken home.

Clients who do not buy much printing may be shocked to learn the cost of going from two-color to four-color process on a small publication. The publications specialist can explain the necessity for four negatives and plates to achieve the color and what these separations and extra press runs cost.

On long press runs, the cost of adding color photos may be very modest on a per copy basis. For example, one large university prints 260,000 copies of a 16-page tabloid for its alumni and others. The basic printing cost in 1991 is $13,400 per issue. Adding 10 color photos costs an additional $1,300, but reader surveys indicate the color is well worth the additional expense.

Who should buy printing?

At some institutions almost everyone gets into the act. Printing should be purchased by the publications office, if there is one, or by the person in the public relations office responsible for maintaining the quality of the institution's public appearance. Unless there is an expert printing buyer in the purchasing office or business office, these are not the places to initiate and specify printing jobs.

The publications office should cooperate closely with the purchasing department, however, in keeping proper records. No printing of any kind should be purchased without a written order. Your business office can help you set up the proper terminology for contracts and establish good buying methods.

Since each printed piece requires a special approach, you cannot buy printing in the same way that other supplies for the college are purchased. "Buying printing" in some ways is a misstatement of the relationship that exists between the publications office and the printer. The printer, the editor, and the designer are jointly engaged in creating a publication, and this is not the same thing as merely buying a service. Frequent contact with a good printer provides an exchange of ideas and suggestions that goes beyond the ordinary relationship of buyer and seller.

Paying the bills

The last step in buying printing is paying the bills. Most printers are honest, but wise business practices require that you carefully check all printing bills. If you had an accurate and detailed estimate of what the job should cost, the first step is to compare the estimate with the final bill. Always insist that your bills be itemized and that you don't receive a lump sum bill for any job. No conscientious printer should object to breaking the bill down into categories such as composition, press-work, author's alterations, paper, binding, and any extra delivery charges.

Let's hope that you and your printer are always the best of friends and never have to argue over prices, delivery time, proofs, and so on. But if you want to be safe, review the Trade Customs printed on the reverse side of many printers' job estimates. Knowing the rules in advance can save you many a headache later.

Chapter 5

The Catalog

One of the most important modern conceptions of a university catalog is that it is a public contract. This fact is frequently overlooked, especially by those who use a catalog for advertising purposes. The prospective student reading a catalog of an institution has a right to assume that its statements are official and authentic. He has the further right to assume that if he should enroll himself at any institution the course of study as announced could be pursued. If one is to assume a reasonable amount of intelligence on the part of the public or of the prospective student one must also assume that a student has a certain vested right in the opportunity announced in the catalog (W. O. Thompson, *The American College Catalog,* 1916).

Not every college publishes an annual report or faculty/staff newsletter, but every college and university in the U.S. issues an official catalog. In many cases this catalog costs more than any other item in the publications budget. Certainly in the eyes of the general public, the catalog is the one printed piece immediately associated with the institution.

Someone has estimated that woodmen cut down tens of thousands of trees every year to produce 80 million college catalogs. These catalogs cost at least $150 million in typesetting and printing expenditures, not to mention editorial, design, proofreading, postage, and handling expenses.

As the most representative publication, the college or university catalog should reflect the heritage, good taste, and dignity of the institution. It should be the product of serious and sustained planning. The product that it describes—higher education—may mean the investment of four years and more than $40,000 for the reader.

In recent years, the catalog has undergone considerable scrutiny by college and university authorities. At some institutions it has become a guinea pig for bizarre experiments, while at others overprotective guardians have refused to consider even the possibility of change.

New answers to old questions have been suggested. For whom is the catalog primarily intended? What is the catalog supposed to accomplish? What should be left to other publications?

The omnibus catalog—something for everyone

Editors know that a publication that tries to be all things to all people may succeed in being very little to anyone. Multipurpose publications aimed at not one or two but a dozen different reading publics seldom serve any purpose well. The catalogs of many institutions can serve as a textbook example of this basic publications error.

For whom is the catalog mainly intended? For prospective students? Faculty and staff members? Enrolled students? Trustees? Registrars at other institutions? Donors and benefactors? Librarians? Lawyers? Some institutions refuse to make these fundamental decisions on primary and secondary audiences. As a result, all those who can impose their views try to twist the catalog to serve their own purpose.

The business manager wants to make sure that the residence qualifications and financial statements are loophole-proof to satisfy any lawyer, even though high school students may be thoroughly baffled by the jargon. Faculty members want to be sure the catalog lists their names, all their degrees, the institutions that granted them, the years in which they were granted, the year they joined the staff, and all their academic titles. The dean or department head insists on listing courses that have not been offered for a decade. The dean of students thinks it imperative to restate the institution's regulations on alcoholic beverages, parking, and cohabitation. And so on through the college hierarchy.

The content of a college catalog can also be determined by what the institution legally has to put in and information that the prospective or enrolled student wants to know. Some years ago, the U.S. Department of Health, Education, and Welfare (now Health and Human Services) mandated that all colleges and universities must include in their catalogs detailed information on such things as minority rights, programs for the handicapped, and financial aid programs. Student groups have also been active in demanding information that once was not found in most college catalogs.

As a result, the college catalog became an omnibus publication. No one sets up a priority or list of objectives, and year by year it balloons to staggering dimensions. One midwestern college even lists all living alumni and their home addresses in its catalog—probably at the suggestion of the alumni director.

To mail these tomes to a 17- or 18-year-old high school student who inquires about your institution verges on the irresponsible. While most of the copies may go to just such a reading public, it is evident that some catalogs were prepared with the interests, pet projects, and reading comprehension level of the professors and deans in mind.

Quite apart from the wisdom of throwing a collection of rules, regulations, lists, course descriptions, and names at a prospective student, it became apparent to many institutions that they could not afford to send a catalog that cost $2 or $3 to every Tom, Dick, and Sally who wrote a post card to the admissions office. An energetic high school senior could write 25 post cards in study hall and include many institutions in which he or she had only a mild interest.

Some institutions, especially the larger universities, have had to exert restraint in giving free sets of catalogs to one and all. One major state university sends complete sets of its graduate and undergraduate catalogs to every high school and public library in the state, selected out-of-state schools, major public libraries around the country, and so on.

It still gets dozens of letters and post cards every week from high schools and libraries far from its natural constituency base. These form letters cost the senders only pennies, but if this university were to respond to every request with a set of catalogs, it would cost more than $7 to print and $3.40 to ship each four-and-a-half-pound package of publications. With 30,000 high schools in the U.S. and thousands of libraries, colleges and universities, school counselors, military bases, and the like, the university would spend an enormous amount of money if it sent catalogs to everyone who asked.

The multipurpose, gray-covered omnibus catalog began to disappear after World War II. New efforts were made to pinpoint the audience, simplify the language, streamline the organization, cut out the deadwood, and trim printing and mailing costs. Mistakes were made. Resistance to change often dies hard on the campus of an institution traditionally devoted to the discovery and dissemination of new ideas.

First, determine the purpose

Those charged with putting out the catalog began their search for a solution to the problem by asking the basic questions: Why are we publishing a catalog? What do we want to say? To whom do we want to say it?

The answer to the first question varied from campus to campus. For some institutions the catalog was the chief recruiting piece. For others it was considered a matter of record and a legal contract. For some it was a campus guide to curricula and courses for current students. If anything is clear about higher education in the U.S., it is that each college and university has its own character, problems, and methods of solving them. The primary purpose of one catalog may be quite different from that of a neighboring institution because of the type of institution, its printing budget, its educational philosophy, or its recruiting practices.

A questionnaire published in *College and University,* the journal of the American Association of Collegiate Registrars and Admissions Officers, asked students to rank in order of importance and usefulness 121 items of information that might be found in college catalogs. The top 25 catalog items in order of their popularity were as follows:

1. admissions procedures and policies;
2. when, where, and how to apply;

3. educational background required for entrance;
4. admission requirements such as aptitude tests;
5. degrees offered;
6. tuition and fees;
7. degree programs;
8. an index;
9. number of units required for degree;
10. special degree programs;
11. admissions requirements for in-state and out-of-state students and foreign students;
12. accreditation;
13. courses—number, title, credit;
14. description of financial aid;
15. explanation of credit system;
16. advanced placement and credit;
17. calendar;
18. eligibility for financial aid;
19. grading system;
20. course description;
21. directory of inquiries;
22. major requirements;
23. payment plans;
24. special programs such as early admission; and
25. course prerequisites.

Only four items (out of 121) elicited so many responses of "no interest" as to warrant leaving them out of a catalog. In order of their unpopularity, they were:

1. listing of faculty's professional employment history;
2. lists of graduates and students;
3. school attended by faculty even if degree was not earned;
4. listing of faculty's rank with date of appointment to that rank.

Alternatives to the omnibus catalog

When the answer to the first question ("Why are we publishing a catalog?") indicated that the omnibus catalog no longer served the purpose originally intended, editors began to consider alternatives. Some institutions developed small, illustrated, concise admissions booklets. Some published parts of the catalog as separate booklets (scholarships and financial aid, ROTC, religious activities, directory of students, and so on). A few produced catalogs for freshmen only, which answered the questions a student might ask before and during the first year.

The larger universities with subordinate colleges and professional schools saw the wastefulness of sending a 1,000-page catalog to a student who was only interested in the 36 pages that described the pharmacy school. They split their complete catalog into individual school catalogs with perhaps a supplementary general information bulletin. They could then answer requests by sending an individualized catalog that might cost 50 cents to print, compared to a complete catalog costing $4 or more. This made it easier for students to find the information they wanted. These universities could also bind a limited number of the separate catalogs into a complete catalog for school officials, counselors, and libraries.

At one time most institutions issued an annual catalog. Many now put out the catalog on a biennial basis. The savings in editorial time, composition, and printing can be substantial. A few colleges and universities went from annual to biennial catalog publication and then backtracked because of faculty protests. Most institutions that made the change heard very few complaints and have realized substantial savings ever since.

Some thought has been given to eliminating costly internal course catalogs completely through the use of computer printout schedule cards, individually tailored to each student. At this point, the production of personal computerized catalogs is still in the experimental stage.

If the catalog is intended mainly for prospective students, as many are, the editors should consult college admissions counselors to see if the publication answers the questions most often asked. Some editors meet with a small panel of high school counselors and teachers to get their side of the picture and obtain a frank evaluation of the college's publications. One New England college brought half a dozen high school people to the campus, chatted with them for several hours, took them to lunch in the student union, and paid for their transportation. The suggestions they received from the cooperating counselors more than repaid the small expense.

Another method, though probably less effective, is to mail questionnaires to high school seniors, teachers, or your own college freshmen to find out what publications were most helpful, what information was missing or slighted, and what problems they encountered in locating the information.

A professional editor does not view the catalog in isolation. If the college also publishes a prospectus, viewbook, or admissions booklet, the editor tries to see how one publication meshes with another, how duplication can be avoided, how similar publications might be combined, or how one publication trying to serve various audiences might better be broken up. The catalog becomes the nucleus of the college's recruiting literature, which may include a financial aid booklet, ROTC pamphlet, career material, religious activities booklet, manuals for principals and teachers, and a student handbook.

Eliminating the nonessentials

For an institution first tackling the catalog problem, the elimination of unnecessary material might be a good beginning. For example, who cares about pages of committee assignments? Likewise lists of enrolled students, recent graduates, and alumni may take up space in the catalog that could be put to better use. Every catalog lists the faculty members by name, but some larger universities no longer list every degree held by every instructor and professor; admissions directors know that such information means nothing to high school students and little to under-graduates. It could be published in a separate directory for less money. Some institutions set a word limit, say 35 words, on course descriptions. How many courses begin with the same tired: "A study of. . ." or "This course intends to. . ."?

Regulations about personal conduct might better be left to the student handbooks that almost all institutions publish. Even a registrar of the "old school" will find it hard to defend the inclusion of behavior codes in the official catalog.

It's hard to describe the information that every catalog should contain because each institution has its own unique needs. We can safely say, however, that a comprehensive college or university catalog should contain all or most of the following elements:

- second-class mailing information;
- table of contents;
- calendar;
- academic calendar;
- general information;
- historical sketch;
- location of institution;
- accreditation;
- admission requirements;
- registration procedures;
- degrees offered;
- expenses;
- financial aid;
- housing;
- libraries and laboratories;
- academic regulations;
- degree requirements;
- student welfare and services;
- student life and activities;
- description of courses;
- officers of administration and instruction; and
- index.

You might also include statements on grounds and buildings; lists of prizes, medals, and awards; enrollment charts; a campus map; a list of faculty members and degrees held; athletic policy; and so on.

Organizing for accessibility

No one but a proofreader reads a catalog from cover to cover. A catalog is mainly a reference work, and the readers should be helped to find their way to the information they want and need. The editor should spend at least as much or more time on organizing the material as on design and typography. The rule of thumb for some editors is that used by newspaper and magazine editors: The information of greatest interest goes in the front. If prospective or enrolled students are the primary audience, put the material they need to know in the front part of the catalog. List of trustees, statistical data, specific scholarship recognition lists, and the like can go in the appendix.

Including the following will make your catalog easier to use and understand:

• *A survey page in the front of the catalog.* This summary describes the type and special circumstances of the institution: public, private, or church related; for men, women, or both; urban or rural setting; liberal arts, technical, university; and so forth.

• *A complete table of contents and index.* It's hard to believe that some colleges still issue a basic reference work such as the catalog without any index at all. To compensate for the prospective student's unfamiliarity with college jargon, the indexer should try to cross-reference common terms in several ways.

• *An honest statement of costs.* Some institutions continue to quote a ridiculously low estimate of costs (room, board, and tuition). Parents who base their budget on such estimates soon learn to revise them upward once the student enrolls. The costs they had expected to pay may go up another 50 percent when they count snacks and extra food, entertainment, haircuts, cosmetics, new clothes for the campus, transportation, club dues, church contributions, additional books and magazines, etc., etc. These items are hard to pin down for any individual, but presenting an honest range of costs will enable parents to make a realistic comparison.

• *A meaningful description of financial aid.* This does not mean page after page of listed named scholarships. Many scholarship directors prefer that the applicants not try for any specific scholarships anyway. They try to match the student's needs and abilities with available scholarships. What is needed is a concise statement of how to apply for a scholarship, a loan, or a part-time job; how much to expect from each; and how to hold onto this aid by meeting certain scholastic requirements.

• *A directory of correspondence.* Such a listing on the inside front or back cover tells students and their parents to whom they should write to get specific information about fraternities and sororities, off-campus housing, financial aid, admissions, ROTC, transcripts, and so on.

• *Typographical devices of various kinds.* These devices, which guide readers to the information they need, might include graded headings, graphs and charts, running heads at the top of the page, perhaps a thumb index for main sections.

Readability

Once your students have found the information they need, will they be able to understand it? The authors of *Catalogues Are for Students, Too* reviewed catalogs from 20 major universities chosen at random. When they applied the Flesch formula for readability to these catalogs, they found scores ranging from 19 to 44 with a mean of 28.6. A Flesch Reading Ease Score of 0 to 30, usually found in scientific and professional journals, is classified as "very difficult." "Difficult" material is rated between 30 and 50 and is found in academic and scholarly periodicals. The typical *Atlantic Monthly* article is rated as "Fairly Difficult" (50 to 60); mass non-fiction, *Time* magazine, and the digests are 60 to 70 and classified as "Standard."

The researchers concluded that only the top 5 percent of the country's adult readers can read the typical college catalog with ease. Instead of writing for high school juniors and seniors, editors apparently believe they are addressing college graduates with several years of postgraduate study. While you need not resort to baby talk and pictographs to tell your story to prospective college students, remember who they are and adjust your writing accordingly.

To improve the readability of your catalog, use common shorter words in place of the esoteric, shorter average sentences and paragraphs, and fewer involved sentence constructions. Define unfamiliar words or list them in a glossary. The high school student may not understand terms such as "core curriculum," "credit hours," "scholastic index," "cumulative grade points," and so forth.

Design

Few institutions still publish the old-fashioned catalog with a cover printed in black ink on gray antique stock. In fact, this once standard combination is now so rare that its use might again attract attention. Editors have gone to brighter paper and inks. Sometimes they use two or more inks and four-color process illustrations. Unfortunately, some colleges have limited their catalog remodeling to "dressing up" the drab cover. The text has remained as dull, disorganized, and distended as it always was.

Some developments in the college catalog field approach the bizarre. One institution used four colors of paper for its catalog: white, pink, light blue, and yellow. The colored stock did not indicate new sections but merely signatures. This rainbow arrangement was unlikely to gain many converts.

The size and type of headings are important. Properly graded display lines can direct the reader to important items. Although the bulk of catalog material will be set in 10 or 8 point type, some types of reference material may well be set in 6 or 7 point since no one will read this from beginning to end.

Differences in readability among the popular typefaces are negligible, but you should use italics only for emphasis and avoid too much boldface; it gives a splotchy appearance to the page. If your catalog is large—and you've already eliminated all nonessentials—try setting it in one of the typefaces that allow the maximum number of characters and words on the line. Without sacrificing readability you can pack more copy into fewer pages.

Some editors, especially those who have gone to the larger page size, such as 8½ by 11, have tried a double- and even triple-column format for text, course descriptions, and faculty listings. They can use a smaller type size on a shorter measure while preserving readability. Such type columning may also eliminate extra white space and allow more characters per inch.

Who's in charge?

We have referred to the individual responsible for issuing the catalog as the editor. Actually many people in many different jobs carry this responsibility on different campuses.

The person in charge of the catalog may be the registrar, public relations director, assistant to the president, dean, college secretary, or the university editor or director of publications. Where the college has established a publications office, it would not seem reasonable to exempt the catalog, the most official and expensive and representative publication in the stable, from such supervision. Of course, the editor would work closely with the registrar, the director of admissions, the deans, and all others concerned.

If your office has the responsibility for issuing the catalog, you will want to make a continuing survey of other college and university catalogs. This creative plagiarism will enable you to borrow the best ideas from your colleagues on other campuses. You will soon learn that no more than two dozen institutions in the country ever contribute anything new or revolutionary in the catalog field. Whether your school catalog is primarily an attractive student recruiting piece or an academic reference work, it stands as the most important part of your publications program. As such it demands continuing efforts to improve its usefulness.

Chapter 6

Recruiting and Career Materials

Some elite colleges, universities, and professional schools still find that one of their greatest chores is to select the lucky few whose applications for admission will be accepted. These new students are drawn from a large pool of hopefuls; perhaps one out of 10 applicants makes the grade.

Far more institutions, however, face a serious shortage of freshman applicants, and the situation will only get worse. Since World War II, higher education in this country has been a growth industry. Enrollments increased almost every year. Those days may be over.

Demographers tell us that the pool of students available for the freshman class of 1991 will be nearly one-third smaller than in 1979. President John Silber of Boston University has written: "By 1995, assuming that Americans continue to go to college at the present rate, both state and independent colleges and universities will be educating 3 million fewer students. Even with extraordinary expansion in continuing education, the deficit cannot be less than 1 million students" (*Straight Shooting: What's Wrong with America and How to Fix It,* 1989).

This decline will not be evenly spread across the nation. The northeastern states will see a falloff of 30 percent of 18-year-olds while the western states will lose only 12 percent. But the shortage of college freshmen will certainly mean that a number of today's colleges and universities will not be around by the year 2000.

The need to provide attractive, honest, readable publications to present the case for attending your institution has never been greater. The survival of your institution may be at stake.

Bodies for the student body are not enough. Every responsible institution wants not just students but outstanding students: students who apply themselves and know their career goals; students with promise who will inspire others, encourage the faculty, and brighten the hearts of alumni directors 20 years from now.

Young men and women who enroll in your institution imagining that college

49

in the 1990s is a picnic or a yearlong joy ride because this was the impression given by your booklets and brochures will be liabilities. They will be taking up valuable dormitory and classroom space, frustrating their professors, and lowering the intellectual level of the classes they choose to attend. Students who stumble onto your campus because they think they can get the professional training your viewbook hints at but your institution does not actually offer will be wasting their time and money and that of many other people.

This chapter covers some of the publications, other than the official catalog, used either directly or indirectly to recruit and interest prospective students. This includes viewbooks, general information booklets, descriptions of career opportunities, and the like.

These range from tiny 2 ½ by 5 miniatures to handsome 9 by 12 books printed in four-color process. Costs range from a few pennies a copy to $2 or more, depending on size and format of the publication, press run, printing process, use of color, and type of paper stock.

We can divide these publications into three categories according to purpose:
• providing vocational or career information;
• providing information about the particular institution—admission requirements and policies, curricula, housing, student activities, financial aid, athletics, religious development, and the like; and
• combining admissions information with career information.

Career information

High school counselors and teachers appreciate up-to-date and objective career booklets. The college or university that can afford to provide such material at no cost or nominal cost will find a ready welcome in most high schools. It will be performing a genuine service to prospective students and their parents and counselors, even though the name of the college appears only on the cover or in the second-class mailing box.

In these career publications, you can mention the special programs and facilities of the institution, but the emphasis should be on the career field. The pictures and text concentrate on what the student does *after* graduation rather than on how he or she prepares for a career during the four years in college.

High schools will not use these booklets unless they are reliable and honest. They should present an accurate assessment of the advantages and disadvantages of the career, the expected need for trained people, special information for women and minorities, and the approximate financial rewards. They can "sell" the career with some enthusiasm, but should not exaggerate. A professionally oriented high school counselor or teacher puts the interests of the students first and will soon recognize and refuse to distribute publications that present a distorted picture.

Even within general areas of instruction such as engineering or journalism, universities specialize in certain fields. Not every engineering school offers accredited programs in every phase of engineering. Some may offer programs approved by the Engineers Council for Professional Development in only two or three fields. A mention of these accredited sequences would be appropriate in a career monograph, but the booklet should cover the range of engineering careers. The engineering school that offers only mechanical and civil engineering should try to present statements from other branches as well: aeronautical, metallurgical, chemical, electrical, mining, industrial, and so on.

The journalism school should explain opportunities in daily and weekly newspaper work, advertising, public relations, radio and TV, magazines, and industrial journalism. This is the kind of vocational literature that high schools are looking for, and the college providing it will win a vote of thanks from high school counselors.

Illustrations for these publications should relate mainly to the careers, not training for careers. A booklet that describes the life of a doctor should not be illustrated with photos of laboratories in the medical school. They should depict what the student does *after* receiving the M.D.—internship, general practice, specialization, house and office calls, hospital work, research, public health.

Editors can often obtain top-quality photographs at little or no cost from professional societies, industrial public relations departments, the government, or commercial sources. For example, a university preparing a booklet on business careers could describe its picture needs in letters to 20 corporate public relations directors and receive a fine selection of glossy prints.

Counselors and teachers are more likely to use these career publications if they are helpful for all students interested in the vocation, rather than just those interested in the particular institution. The college or university that has produced such a publication is showing that it doesn't claim to be all things to all people, but is willing to put its cards on the table, present the choices objectively, and provide help to students—whether they are potential applicants or not.

Sometimes this type of publication is not easy to sell to deans and department heads in the particular field of study. They may urge you to include more material about the institution's program—curricula and course content, tabulations of books in the library, descriptions of new laboratories. Some academicians may think it a waste of college funds to publicize careers for which the institution does not prepare students. The testimonials of high school counselors and college admissions directors may help convince them that a policy of providing complete and accurate career information will build more acceptance and good will in the long run than "hard sell" publications about campus facilities and programs.

Information about the institution

The second type of admissions publication is frankly concerned with the particular college or university itself. It is often distributed along with career booklets. These admissions publications provide some of the same information found in the general catalog but in a less formal and more attractive way. They are designed to answer the most common questions asked by prospective students and to furnish concise statements of what the high school senior or junior needs to know about your institution.

The prospectus or general information booklet is the standard publication in this category. In its original format the "viewbook" suffered from a number of drawbacks. Years ago when administrators saw the need to provide a warmer, more colorful picture of college life, they hit upon publishing a sort of photo album. These early efforts were little more than picture books.

The editors made the mistake of relying too much on photographs. Even outstanding pictures cannot carry the ball alone. A photograph can show grief, joy, anticipation, or excitement, but it can't tell the whole story.

The best prospectuses and general information booklets combine good photographs with well-written text. They may also use graphs and charts. While you still see a few of the old-fashioned pictures-and-captions viewbooks, this probably means that those in charge have not analyzed their usefulness or invited prospective students or counselors to assess their value.

No two general information booklets contain the same elements, but here are some of the most frequently used components:
- a discussion of college choice;
- a statement about the college or university;
- the courses of study;
- admission requirements;
- housing;
- a campus map;
- costs and financial aid;
- ROTC programs;
- student services;
- campus activities;
- religious opportunities;
- accreditation;
- athletics;
- student government;
- social life;
- the academic calendar;
- a directory for correspondence;
- a glossary of college terms; and
- regulations.

The same integrity and honesty that govern the career booklets should govern this recruitment piece. The publication should reflect the institution in its best light but not in a false light. Every college can tell about its special character, its distinguished faculty members, its unique programs, its particular emphasis. It need not present itself under false colors to attract the type of student who should be enrolling in the institution.

This need for honesty is especially true when it comes to college costs. Some institutions apparently use as estimates of costs the expenses of a poverty-stricken freshman living in a garret on popcorn and water, wearing Salvation Army handouts, and listening to a crystal set for entertainment. At the very least, a college should present some range of costs for such items as room, board, entertainment, extra food, clothing, books, and the like. As it stands now, the college using realistic cost figures is penalized because parents and students think that they could never afford such expenses. They soon discover by the middle of the freshman year that they are actually paying as much or more at some college that offered misleading cost estimates.

Standards of honesty should likewise apply to all the publications issued with the college imprint. One month one of the authors got two booklets from the same institution. The first was directed toward prospective students and the second toward alumni. The photographs in the student booklet led you to believe that the oldest building on campus must have been dedicated last year. Scholarly looking professors lectured small classes of bright-eyed students. Other students hungry for knowledge performed experiments in modern laboratories and consulted books and journals in the spacious university library.

The second publication painted a far different picture. If the prospective student bulletin depicted life at Utopia U., the alumni appeal might have come from Catastrophe College. Classes were apparently taught in converted army barracks. A single light bulb on a bare cord provided barely enough illumination to enable the students to decipher the texts. Professors stooped to avoid bumping into exposed steam pipes in their makeshift basement offices, which they shared with half a dozen other scholars. There was standing room only in the library, while the chemistry lab looked like it had been equipped with toy chemistry sets, rejects from last year's Christmas supply.

No one objects to some tailoring of publications to fit different audiences; however, we must say that this institution overstepped the ethical boundaries. Had the mailings been switched, the university would have gotten neither new students nor new dollars. A college or university cannot at one and the same time be well-equipped and ramshackle, picturesque and dilapidated, outstanding and in danger of losing its accreditation because of academic deficiencies.

A college or university is not a circus or road show. It stays in one place and seldom moves its campus to another location. If it tries to camouflage its real situation with glossy publications and misleading publicity, high school counselors, parents, businessmen, and prospective students will begin to discount whatever the institution says about itself. It will attract only the credulous or naive, and they will probably be disenchanted after a visit to the campus or a semester in the institution's classrooms.

During the 1960s and '70s, another element entered the picture. Various agencies of the federal government—such as the Veterans Administration, HEW's Office for Civil Rights, the State Department, and the Department of Education—demanded the inclusion of specific statements in college and university catalogs and recruiting materials.

Besides the verbal sleight-of-hand artists who sometimes edit college viewbooks, the cliche experts get their hands on many prospectuses. Their supply of superlatives is inexhaustible. When Alan G. Schreihofer examined 26 college viewbooks, he was able to lift enough quotations to produce the following description of Unimaginative University. It appeared in *Pride* magazine, published by the American College Public Relations Association (a CASE predecessor organization). Only the names have been changed to protect the guilty:

> You, as a serious-minded college prospect, have an important task before you, namely, deciding which college to attend. We hope that you will seriously consider Unimaginative and strive to be one of the limited number of carefully selected students with outstanding secondary school records who will receive the advantages of a liberal arts education at Unimaginative.
>
> Unimaginative offers you an education having both breadth and depth; a broad base of knowledge as well as highly specialized training in your chosen field. Your Unimaginative education will give you deep-reaching intellectual experiences, a fuller insight into human life, and a better understanding of yourself and the world in which you live. Your admission will open the way to four years of adventure, excitement, and wonderful new horizons.
>
> The happy, scenic home of Unimaginative is in a sea of pines in the heart of the far-famed Wattahoochee Valley. The well-equipped educational plant sprawls over 110 acres of spacious lawns with winding, tree-covered walks, which form a gracious background for the traditional, white-columned Georgian buildings.
>
> There is a fine, carefully selected library with a quiet, relaxing atmosphere that makes it a pleasant place for comfortable study.
>
> The social center of campus is the ultra-modern student union, which has ample room and facilities and is an ideal location for activities. It has a cozy snack bar as well as an attractive, well-appointed dining hall with wholesome and delicious meals that make the dining hour an anticipated pleasure each day.
>
> You will spend your happy, fruitful college years in warm, tasteful residence halls fully equipped with the latest in modern living. The bright and cheerful rooms are pleasantly furnished with early American furniture, and there are many large, attractive lounges.
>
> The strong point of any university is its faculty. Unimaginative boasts a distinguished faculty with stimulating professors who are men of ideals and convictions about the big questions of life. Small classes and a low student/faculty ratio have proved helpful in bringing about a close, personal relationship between faculty and student. Your teachers will be concerned with you as an individual; they will become your friends. Yes, Unimaginative is one big happy family in the fellowship of learning. Here you will make loyal and trusted friends who will mean much to you throughout life.
>
> A physical education program designed to benefit everyone, not merely a few, is made possible through fine athletic facilities and a well-

balanced athletic program. There is a wealth of sports equipment of all kinds in the magnificent new field house and well-equipped gymnasium. These sporting activities will teach you valuable lessons in sportsmanship, courage, and skillful achievement.

Extracurricular activities abound and prove a valuable supplement for classroom work by encouraging growth in creativeness, confidence, social adjustment, and leadership. Well-organized social programs provide a wide variety of wholesome recreational activities and the camaraderie that comes from a closely knit group participating together.

Admission/career information

Some admissions publications include both career and specific admission information. In this case the institution will probably discuss only those careers for which it prepares students. It may wish to include sample curricula or at least indicate what the student will take during the freshman year. Some admissions directors are convinced that most high school seniors have little interest in what they must take as juniors or seniors. They are curious about what is coming next, what they'll be studying as freshmen, but after this they will take whatever they need to get a degree in their chosen major.

Other admissions publications include special booklets outlining career opportunities for women, the freshman program of study, college costs, ROTC, guides for high school counselors, profiles of freshman classes, and so on.

The editors who produce first-rate admissions materials are usually the ones who work closely with the institution's admissions staff. They are the men and women who regularly visit high schools, talk with the teachers and counselors, answer student questions, and chat with parents. To ignore their advice in preparing admissions materials would be foolhardy. A good working relationship between the admissions director and the publications director is essential.

Chapter 7

Publications for Fund Raising

S ome years ago, at a workshop on development techniques, an administrator of a large midwestern university told the following story: A little old lady
in Chicago had written to the university asking for information about the
institution. They put her on the mailing list and heard nothing more from her.
When she died about 10 years later, she left the university $250,000 for its school
of music. As far as anyone knew, she had never visited the campus, never talked
to any fund raiser, never received a personal letter, never attended the institution,
never had any relatives who went there. Her only contact was the infrequent publications she received.

As a practical matter, no institution can plan a program of development publications around the faint hope of attracting the attention of a "little old lady" some-
where. What, then, *is* the purpose of development publications? Put in the simplest
and narrowest terms, the ultimate purpose of all development publications is to
raise money. In a wider view, development literature includes any printed material
that informs or attracts the attention of foundations, government agencies, corporations, alumni, or other individuals who may be in a position to advance the
cause of the institution.

"Everything we print—everything we send out—from the alumni magazine to
the course catalog is in a very real sense a development publication," a successful fund-raising professional told an attentive audience of college administrators.
In fact, we can carry this idea to its logical conclusion and suggest that *everything*
an institution does will ultimately affect its ability to attract future financial support.

Fund-raising publications may range in scope from a single, extremely detailed
presentation delivered to a foundation or individual to a million or more copies
of a rotogravure supplement printed in the Sunday edition of the *New York Times*.
In this chapter we focus on printed materials sent to a sizable group, but add some
comments about the custom-made presentation.

Development publications may be either direct appeals or indirect, long-range
materials.

Direct appeals

Direct pieces describe a specific problem and ask for specific amounts of money to solve that problem. For example, a college may be raising funds for a new library. It may send an appeal to alumni and individual donors, perhaps to foundations, corporations, or the local community.

The appeal describes the problem: lack of adequate study space, the need for books, facilities, and so forth. The program for the future is described with an artist's sketch or architect's rendering, floor plans, perhaps even photographs of a scale model if the project warrants it. At the end is the price tag—a summary of the total cost of the new library. This is usually broken down into bite-sized pieces, often called a "shopping list," to enable as many donors as possible to receive recognition for their gifts. Rooms, lounges, book collections, specific equipment can be "sold" in this manner.

This is the direct approach. You have a problem; you have a solution; and to make the solution come to fruition, you are asking for money. This is the most common type of fund-raising piece, and it can take many forms, some of which we will treat later.

Indirect, long-range materials

The indirect development piece is a long-range, interest-arousing publication that is shooting for substantial and continuing support. It is meant to make a variety of important people aware of institutional achievement and goals: what the institution is doing, what it has done in the past, what it hopes to do in the future. Many indirect development publications never mention anything as mundane as gifts, bequests, and endowments. The annual report of a college can be seen as a long-range development piece, and an introductory message from the president may stress the necessity for increasing funds. The indirect piece does not usually mention exact amounts.

Many development officers consider every printed piece produced for their institution to be a "development" piece. To the extent that all public relations or academic materials affect the institution's image, this is true. However, to attempt to build into each and every pamphlet, catalog, and folder a development message would not only be a waste of high-priced time, but might also backfire to the detriment of the entire public relations program. We have even seen "proper forms for bequests" printed in undergraduate catalogs and can only wonder at the response these must bring from 17-year-old readers.

Spend money to make money—but wisely

More money is spent, and with fewer budgeting qualms, on fund-raising pieces than on any other type of printed material produced by a college or university.

The axiom "It takes money to make money" has been widely recognized; in fact, it's been swallowed hook, line, and sinker by most college development staffs and administrators.

We would be the last to dispute the fact that it costs money to turn out any well-written, well-designed, and well-printed publication. The question is, how *much* money does it take?

We believe that the same basic rules of competitive buying and good taste should apply to all publications. We have seen no research to prove that a publication costing $5 a copy *always* does a better job than one produced for 95 cents. Spending a lot of money for slick artwork, luxurious paper, and premium printing won't change drab ideas into a brilliant brochure; but spending enough money wisely can increase the effectiveness of good ideas.

In a random survey of some two dozen development brochures, we found that more than half used die-cut or embossed covers. Process color was used either inside or on the covers of seven pieces, and such devices as affixed gold seals, fold-outs, and pockets for enclosures were much in evidence. The paper used for these brochures was, in all cases, extra heavy No. 1 stock and often deckle-edged. One piece had six different papers plus a half-sheet tissue wraparound. Production processes included silk screen, gold ribbon stamping, and blind embossing.

In all of the brochures, the printing quality was far above the average of other college publications. Even if you consider only the obvious production costs, the most common type of college development brochure adds up to a very expensive piece of printing. Multiply this by the thousands of institutions actively seeking funds, and you have a veritable bonanza for consultants and firms that specialize in this area.

Sad to say, the quality of content and design in the majority of development pieces we have seen comes nowhere near matching the materials used in their production. Instead of solid quality and good taste, many pieces are only ostentatious examples of conspicuous consumption. Not a few otherwise carefully managed colleges have mistaken flashiness for attractiveness and graphic experimentation for sound design.

About the only rule consistently followed in fund-raising literature is that of printing everything in at least 12 point type because wealthy prospects are presumed to be old with poor eyesight.

Harold Seymour, in his very wise and witty book *Designs for Fund-Raising,* makes a plea for moderation in design: "Designers should have fun, and trade medals at the professional meetings for their cute and clever ideas. But the really good ones never forget that their best audiences are bifocal and allergic to strange effects and to change."

The importance of a coordinated publications program

A major fund-raising campaign is an all-out commitment by an institution of time, money, and talent. A successful campaign requires a well-planned and coordinated publications program to support all of the efforts of the fund-raising office. Quite often, before any major development brochures are published, the tone of the campaign is set through the upgrading and redesigning of the institution's general publications. This is particularly useful when the campaign is keyed in with a centennial celebration or some other historical date.

Often, the institution has a graphic device designed especially for the campaign. This device is used on the catalog, stationery, business forms, and mailing labels, as well as all other printed work. Indeed, the launching of a fund campaign often provides a long-awaited opportunity for the publications editor to put a new face on shopworn catalogs. Existing publications are too often neglected in planning and implementing a development campaign. An attractive and coordinated design system can be used not only for publications but also for promotional items such as displays, flags, automobile stickers, directional campus signs, and numerous bookstore items. Spread across many uses, the talent of a top-flight designer is a wise investment in kicking off a fund campaign.

Professional fund raisers will tell you that by far the largest percentage of money in any fund drive comes from a very few persons and that these contributions are almost always solicited personally by friends or campaign volunteers. Nevertheless, printed materials for a fund drive serve an important purpose. Just the process of putting together a statement of institutional aims often clarifies and solidifies the thinking of both faculty and administration. Second, the campaign literature tells the fund-raising volunteer or solicitor exactly what the college hopes to do. While we can't expect immediate direct action from a printed piece, the printed piece can be a useful tool at all stages of a development drive.

The case statement

Preceding the major brochure or case book in most campaigns is a case statement. This is usually a comprehensive and thoroughly documented review of an institution's development history, current problems, specific goals, and suggested programs for advancement. The case statement serves a number of purposes in the development program. It can be used internally to inform faculty and staff of the development program needs and purposes and to solicit their constructive comments and support. This means that everyone in the institution is speaking the same language and has had a chance to participate in molding the campaign goals.

Occasionally, the case statement serves as the early campaign planning piece, and a later development brochure (the case book) grows out of it. At other times, the statement and the brochure are developed together. A number of large universities produce the statement first as a photocopied document, which is then circulated internally. The high points of this working copy are used in the brochure.

The case book

Almost every campaign requires a single comprehensive publication that establishes the theme and presents the total picture. Sometimes called the "case book," the mission of this brochure, as described by one development professional, is to establish the "proper climate for giving." The case book is usually constructed around the following five-point outline:

1. The "cause" or the theme of the campaign is established. It is always something greater and more important than the immediate money goals. The titles of a number of representative development brochures give you an idea of some of the typical themes: "Commitment to the Future," "Investment in a Greater Tomorrow," "Assignments for the Ages," "Assure the Future of a Noble Past," "The Search for Knowledge," "A Program for the Future," "The Edge of Greatness," "On Looking Inward," "The Great Awakening," and so on. Many brochure titles sound like TV soap operas.

You will notice that the telling point of these themes is "tomorrow." They are also concerned with education, the progress of humanity, and, of course, excellence. In other words, these are causes that are greater than the need for a dormitory or a library.

Note that the following short paragraph from a major university's annual development report looks far beyond the mundane needs of the campus: "As the world around us continues to change, it challenges us with new problems. Therefore we must continually develop our faculty, student body, research, and facilities to meet those challenges, or else we will fail to fulfill our obligations to society as well as to our founders."

2. Having established a lofty theme, the institution explains itself and gives its credentials for being the agency that can best promote the theme. The second section of the brochure must establish the educational progressiveness of the institution, its past history of academic accomplishments and pioneering research, its record of striving toward excellence.

3. The brochure copy moves on to make it clear that the institution has a plan for the future. It does not intend to rest on its laurels. To further this great cause for humanity, for progress, for the future, it is ready to lay down a carefully drawn blueprint. It knows where it is going, and it plans to do something.

4. "We tried, but . . ." could be the heading of the fourth part of the brochure. After showing that the institution has the pedigree for performance, that it has a studied plan for the future, it must establish without a doubt that a serious problem is preventing it from reaching its goal. And this problem is, not surprisingly, insufficient money.

At this point in the brochure, the institution should emphasize that it has worked hard to solve its financial problems. It must show clearly that it has struggled valiantly and not unsuccessfully to raise faculty salaries, provide much needed science labs, build a new library, modernize Old Main, construct residence halls, and strengthen the research program.

5. In the wind-up segment of the brochure, the institution turns with confidence to its friends to help solve its problem. Some brochures leave it at that; others go into specific details: dollars needed for raising faculty salaries, building a new library, constructing dormitories, or expanding scientific facilities.

In a nutshell, this publication takes the basic five-point editorial approach used for many fund-raising brochures:

1. the theme;
2. past performance;
3. the plan;
4. the problem; and
5. the solution.

The editorial mood throughout the case book should be one of confidence, anticipating success. It should make it clear to prospective supporters that the success of the project is not only probable but self-evident.

Other printed materials, which sometimes surround the major case statement or brochure, may include a volunteer's kit, which gives special instructions for solicitation or holds a variety of other materials such as special gift folders, bequest information, and memorial opportunities.

In addition to the major development brochure, other printed materials support a total development program. Among the most useful of these are the so-called "service" pieces. These are usually simple folders presenting carefully researched information on estate planning, insurance programs, bequests, and other aspects of philanthropic planning. Often these documents are either written by lawyers or carefully checked by them to be sure the information is clear and accurate.

Grant proposals

An onerous but important task faced by most development staffs is the writing of grant proposals. This job is usually shared by the development writer and the primary professor. Whoever writes the proposal, certain basic rules prevail. Here are some suggestions for the staff member facing this challenge:

1. Put yourself in the position of the person who will be reading your proposal, and try to hear your words from his or her point of view.

2. Do your final proofing and editing on a full printout of your material, not on a computer screen. In order to check for accuracy and avoid repetition, you need to be able to shuffle back and forth among the pages.

3. Make time—uninterrupted, quiet, concentrated time—to read the final draft of your proposal, front to back, before sending it out.

4. Ask yourself these questions:

• Does this proposal effectively convey what I wish the recipient to know?

• Is the overall picture I have drawn of my institution one that inspires confidence in our goals and in the competence and efficiency of each faculty member mentioned in the report?

• Have I stressed the important, worthwhile, and attention-getting accomplishments of the faculty and research personnel?

• Is each project worth mentioning, or do some come across as basic work?

• In merging various portions of other documents into this report, have I accidentally repeated myself?

- If important information needs to be reiterated, have I done so in a fashion that emphasizes rather than simply repeats?
- Is there anything negative in the proposal that would be better left unsaid?
- Does the budget page, which will be scrutinized by the prospective grantor, accurately reflect and emphasize our most important needs? Does it contain any items that do not contribute to the true financial picture?
- Have I given the recipient of this proposal all the information needed to make a decision on further funding?
- Have I inadvertently raised doubts as to the use made of previous funds, the efficient use of future funds, or even the necessity for further funding?
- Have I convinced the grantor that the goals of my institution are goals he or she endorses?

Other development pieces

A large eastern university published a successful service piece in the form of a record book for vital personal information. This piece has been widely distributed to lawyers and trustees of estates as well as potential donors. The booklet provides space for an individual to fill in information about personal history, birth and marriage documentation, Social Security, and other important numbers; medical history; and a complete inventory of stocks, bonds, insurance, real estate, and other assets. It was designed small enough so that it would fit conveniently into a safe-deposit box.

Other publications used successfully by a number of institutions outline the tax advantages of giving and describe a variety of estate planning programs that work to the advantage of both donor and institution.

Almost all estate planning or service publications contain suggested wording for making gifts or bequests, such as the following:

Suggested Wording to Make a Gift
Or Bequest to Ivy Halls University

1. *Outright gift during your life:* "I hereby give, transfer, and deliver to Ivy Halls University, in the City of Utopia, the sum of $_____ [or other appropriately described property] to be used for the benefit of Ivy Halls University in such manner as the Board of Trustees thereof may direct."

2. *Unconditional bequest in your will:* "I give, devise, and bequeath to Ivy Halls University, in the City of Utopia, the sum of $_____ [or other appropriately described property] which may be expended for the general purposes of Ivy Halls University."

3. *Contingent bequest in your will:* ". . . If any of the above-named beneficiaries should predecease me, then I give, devise, and bequeath the property, real or personal, which said beneficiary or beneficiaries would have received if they had sur-

vived me, to Ivy Halls University, in the City of Utopia, for the general purposes of Ivy Halls University."

4. *Bequest of residue in your will:* "I give, devise, and bequeath to Ivy Halls University, in the City of Utopia, all the rest of my property, real and personal, for such purposes as the Board of Trustees thereof may determine."

The annual fund

Among the direct financial appeals conducted by colleges and universities, the most universal is the annual fund. Like the national campaigns of social service agencies, annual giving campaigns are faced with a number of inescapable economic considerations. An annual fund is primarily a direct mail operation. A large number of persons must be solicited, the average contribution is small, and the percentage of contributors must be as great as possible.

One of the most successful approaches to this problem has been the three-piece package—letter, folder, and business-reply envelope. The reply envelope may be the most important of these as it makes it easy for the contributor to insert a check and return it to the proper address. Most professional fund raisers agree that the business-reply envelope pays its way. The institution pays only for actual returns, and eliminating the hunt for a stamp helps get the envelope off an old grad's desk and into the mail.

Alumni appeal letters are not usually personalized, but are addressed "Dear Alumnus," "Fellow Graduate," or some other variation. Tests have shown that the extra expense of first-class mailing produces little if any extra revenue. Some institutions supply first-class, hand-stamped reply envelopes, but usually only for a few small and very special lists.

An economical direct mail solicitation may be a four-page folder packing a lot of information into a small area. The idea is to condense the copy to a minimum and send the piece with a personal letter that invites the recipient to ask for more information. In fund-raising materials, it's often a mistake to spell out everything in detail, because at some point the large donor is going to insist upon some personal contact.

To squeeze the most out of each mailing, the reply envelope should do more than just carry the check back to the institution. It should also sell the giving idea. Often the prospect throws away the letter and brochure and puts the reply envelope in the stack of bills to be paid at the beginning of the month. If the reply envelope doesn't have a reminder message on the flap or back, the prospect who has forgotten his or her charitable intentions by bill-paying time may just toss it in the wastebasket.

Some universities leave space on the back of the annual appeal envelope for the alumnus to fill in a personal news item for the alumni magazine.

Phonathons are an important part of most annual funds. A beginner might think you can do a phonathon simply by recruiting a bunch of enthusiastic students, setting up phone banks, and watching them all call alumni. But one large university, which raises more than $1 million a year through this method, also uses 19 different pieces of printed phonathon materials.

Other development publications might include campaign workers' handbooks, fund progress reports, gift reports (listings of contributors), dinner programs, dedication brochures, and campaign newsletters. Special groups such as century clubs or college associates may also need printed materials from time to time.

No matter how widespread your development publications efforts may be, they should be treated as a coordinated package in design and editorial direction. Unlike many other college publications that have constantly changing audiences, development pieces, particularly alumni materials, are sent year after year to the same groups. Going all out on one brochure while you continue to send out the same old alumni magazine does not make good public relations sense.

Every single piece of printing that bears the name of your institution is part of its total impression. With a little advance planning and good taste, each publication can make a significant contribution to your development program.

Chapter 8

Direct Mail

E very night when I get home, there's a little pile of mail waiting for me. I used to think I'd find something wonderful in the pile, but I never do (Andy Rooney).

Direct mail has been described as anything you mail to people you don't know, who haven't asked for what you're sending, who won't know what it is after they get it, and who will often throw it away before they read it. Despite these handicaps, direct mail promotion continues to grow and to produce results. Surprisingly, most people do open their mail, and if your message catches their eye and their interest, they will respond.

In the college and university field, direct mail includes pieces sent out for student recruitment, fund raising, alumni drives, adult education courses, conferences and workshops, and public information announcements. Direct mail publications can range in form from elaborate four-color brochures to the hard-working post card. Letters, self-mailers, tabloid newspapers, posters, folders, and many other forms are used to try to communicate directly through the mail with an elusive audience.

For any institution, large or small, the most important single use of direct mail is for fund raising. Virginia Carter Smith wraps up this use of direct mail in the following A to Z checklist (adapted from "The ABCs of Raising Money by Mail," CASE CURRENTS, June 1978):

A. Remember that no rules work 100 percent of the time. Because your own constituency differs from every other, you can learn most from your own successes and failures. To do this, keep accurate records on each mailing.

B. We're competing for our reader's time. Picture your graduate getting home from work. Wants a cold drink. Remembers that the refrigerator is broken. Kids rush up. Television blares. Then he or she picks up the mail. If you are lucky, your letter will be opened, but the recipient takes only a few seconds to decide whether to read it. It becomes vitally important that you grab the person in those few seconds.

C. If your mail *is* opened, your next concern is whether it's read—*and acted upon.* Having it read is not enough.

D. The best prospects in direct mail are "former customers"—or, in our case, former givers—and others like them in demographics. Pursue your former givers. Also—with a separate, tailored approach—go after people similar in age, geographic location, college major, occupation, income level, or whatever. This will pay off better than going after dissimilar groups.

E. For best results, segment your prospects. Don't consider them one big mass. Analyze them by dollar-level gifts, frequency of prior gifts, school/college affiliation, major, length of time since graduation, geographic location, and so on. This lets you mail to subgroups in a more personal way.

F. *A letter is the single most important piece you can use in any direct mail effort.* Because of this, your letter should look like a letter. Use typewriter type (not copy that looks typeset), and make the type large enough to be easily read. Be sure it carries a signature, even though it's printed. Monarch size letters (7-1/4 by 10½) seem to work best for big donors. (Even smaller notepaper has worked well for some major charities.) For mass appeals, 8½ by 11 generally draws best.

G. Salutations of some kind are better than none. You might use "Dear Beloiter," "Dear Alumnus/a," "Dear Carolina Graduate," "Dear Member of the Class of 1935." You can use a headline-type salutation on a letter, but consider breaking it up into three or four short lines, placed on the left. This makes it look like a salutation.

H. When you use the letterhead of a volunteer, also mail in an envelope with his or her cornercard. Do not mix volunteer stationery and a college or university envelope. But beware of third-class bulk mailing regulations. If you use a volunteer's envelope, you can't use the college's bulk permit.

I. In writing your letter, write to just one person. Use a conversational style with short words, short paragraphs. Don't hesitate to restate important points; your reader may only read part of the letter. Focus on two groups of motivations: (1) altruism, idealism, and desire to improve conditions and (2) obligation, ego gratification, and gratitude. Outline the need to be met. Tell how your institution is meeting the need. Get the reader personally involved. Establish a close link between his or her support and accomplishing the goal. Show what his or her gift can accomplish. *Ask for the contribution.* Suggest an amount if possible. Tell how to make out the check. State a time limit that issues a call to action.

J. Fit the length of your letter to your message. Make the letter long enough to state the case—and no longer. "Likely givers" will read long letters. Nongivers won't, so shorter letters are probably better for them.

K. Bear in mind the power of the P.S. Readership surveys show that it's often the "most read" feature of a letter. The P.S. gives letters a personal touch. Some experts recommend having the letter signer handwrite the P.S. if it's under 25 words; use the typewriter for a longer P.S. Use this spot for a quick restatement of the case for support and/or a "call to action."

L. If you plan a series of letters in an annual fund campaign, develop a common theme and find ways to say the same things differently. Even if people don't give, make them feel good about having read the letter and make them feel good about themselves. Make them eager to read your next installment. On the other hand, each letter must stand on its own. You can't expect many readers to remember details from a previous letter.

M. In writing your letter, translate "product features" (more books for the library, additional scholarships, or whatever) into "donor benefits" (build stronger university, educate new leadership for society, make your degree mean more, increase your prestige). Use the letter for personal, emotional appeals. If appropriate, put facts, details, pictures in an accompanying brochure.

N. Consider using a "lift letter." Direct mail marketers use this extra letter—usually a single, smaller page—to convince those who may be wavering. It often increases sales by as much as 25 percent. Originally the lift letter used the "frankly I'm puzzled" approach, expressing surprise that the prospective customer would reject such an obviously good deal. You might adapt the lift letter. For example, suppose you are soliciting gifts for a new building or a named professorship. Include, along with the mail letter and other materials, a special memo to the president from a beloved emeritus professor. Reproduce in handwriting on the outside of the memo, "Here's a message that you will find of interest." Or in a mailing encouraging new members to join the President's Club, use a note from a prominent graduate who has already made a commitment.

O. Color? Color seems to help in most everything, but we don't know which colors. There seems to be no consistency. One expert says that older folks prefer cool colors (blue or green instead of red). Another suggests yellow as a positive and acceptable color. Still another direct mail authority consults promotions of the fashion industry to get the "in" colors for the year.

P. Commercial direct mailers have found that "the bigger the better" when it comes to the accompanying brochure. They have also been successful with lots of small insertions.

Q. Individualize and personalize as much as possible. Well-organized class agent systems work because of involvement and personalization. Agents themselves get involved and give. Then they are more effective with their classmates because they personalize their letters. Even a handwritten P.S. by a class agent makes an appeal more appealing.

R. Copies of letters with handwritten message printed on or with a note attached ("We haven't heard from you yet, and there are only three weeks left in this fund year") can pull up to 80-90 percent of the original mailing.

S. To call attention to a special paragraph(s) in your letter, use a second color. Other possibilities: underlining, indentation, all caps.

T. Here's an idea that not everybody will agree with but that does work. Ask for a second gift from those who have already given. Use the same mailing as to nondonors but with a hanger acknowledging the previous gift and making a pitch for another.

U. "Any piece of mail will do better if put in an envelope." Most direct mail experts agree on that point, and the rule holds even in situations where a secretary opens the mail. When mailed to an office address, fund-raising mailings do better in a standard envelope (No. 10 or monarch) without gimmicks. For mailings to alumni, parents, and friends at their homes, experiment with other sizes—larger booklet envelopes or smaller invitation-size envelopes. Use envelope stock of good enough quality to arrive in good shape. Rips and tears on the envelope give a bad impression.

V. Often window envelopes turn out to be the most cost-effective carrier. You can then put your label on the response card or reply envelope flap. This makes it easier for the respondent to answer and makes the donor's name and address readable. An exception: When you're mailing to a high-status group, put the address on the envelope as in a standard letter.

W. Most of us can't afford first-class mail except for gift club-level donors. Use attractive commemorative stamps for them. With whatever class mail, a stamp pulls better than a meter tape and a meter tape pulls better than an indicia. Many mailing houses use metering machines to seal your envelopes so you can get your third-class nonprofit mail metered at no additional cost. Reproducing in typewriter type the letter signer's name over the cornercard can kick up response slightly.

X. Reply envelopes are a must in an effective direct mail package. Make it easy for the donor. Leave enough space for easy writing or attach the graduate's computer label to the pledge portion of the envelope. Use the reply envelope copy to call the reader's attention back to the theme or message of your letter. Consider a color for the reply envelope that blends with your mailing.

Y. Experts debate the merits of paying postage on the reply envelope. It probably pays to affix a stamp on the reply envelope for donor club members when you seek memberships or renewal. This says, "I know I am going to hear from you, and I'm willing to pay for your reply." Some experts suggest using a plain, unstamped reply envelope for small but steady donors, medium-sized donors, and all donors who get their mail at business addresses. Small, occasional, or "hardly-ever" donors should get regular business-reply envelopes (the kind with lots of lines on the front). If the latter two kinds of segmentation are impossible, the trend is to plain, unstamped reply envelopes.

Z. Test, test, test. No big-time commercial mailer would launch a campaign without first testing several versions of a direct mail package. Shifts in color, size of the pieces, wording of the letter, type of postage—all can influence returns. In testing, change only one element at a time so that you will know what is causing the difference in response.

Who should receive your direct mail?

The only reason for sending direct mail material is to get someone to do something. Before they can act, however, they must receive your message, read it, understand it, and be motivated by it.

The first step in achieving results with direct mail is to select your audience carefully. Beg, borrow, buy, or compile yourself the best possible mailing list. This is particularly important today when the cost for postage can run more than the cost of printing your direct mail piece. And assemble your mailing list before you go to the printer with your publications layout. You may find that the size and location of your audience call for a revision of your production plans. In any event, good mailing lists are the most important part of any direct mail campaign.

Before you put any promotional catalog, brochure, or folder into production, determine the ideal audience for the program. Once you have done this, you face a much more difficult task—deciding how to reach this audience.

If your institution is offering a seminar on one aspect of metallurgical engineering, you know that the audience will be limited to metallurgical engineers. These people belong to professional societies, they are licensed by the state, they have frequent conventions. They can be found.

If the program is a concert, however, the interested audience is much wider and harder to pin down. Your mailing list should include groups who have shown some interest in the past—subscribers to concert series, radio program guides, and record clubs, for example. Your mailing net is wider, and the percentage of active responses will be smaller.

Reaching by mail a selective audience for adult education offerings presents a real challenge. Theoretically, this is an area with something of interest for everyone, but practically speaking, only a small portion of the mass audience has the time, the money, and the motivation to take a course. Experience has shown that former adult education students are the best source of new students. These students will also provide you with a profile of the receptive audience for your continuing education programs.

Unfortunately, once you have developed this profile of the type of person you want to reach, there are no mailing lists labeled "adult education prospects." If you know where many of your prospective students live, you can use a geographical scatter-shot type of mailing with some results. The results of these mailings in an attempt to reach a large and vague audience are usually inconclusive at best.

Today, many direct mail lists are developed, maintained, and generated through the use of computer information systems. Properly programmed, a computer can greatly improve the speed, accuracy, and selectivity of all your institution's mailings, whether for fund raising, alumni events, or sale of football tickets.

The best way to develop a mailing list for a general interest program is to build your own. This means screening out of a mass audience an interested group of manageable size. Some institutions use advertisements in local newspapers to reach a mass audience. They put together a basic mailing list through resulting phone inquiries and coupons. Kept up-to-date and classified for special interests, this list becomes more valuable every year.

What should you say?

Write your head, blurbs, and opening sentences so that they command attention and arouse interest in the main copy. Don't wait until the last paragraph to put across that big point. Wastebaskets are filled every day with fine ideas that never get read.

Make full use of format, typography, color, and illustrations to arrest the attention of the reluctant reader.

After you have reached your public, you must somehow stimulate action. This second problem is even more difficult because you must overcome the great dead weight of public inertia. You want your readers to respond to your message in some way—even if it is only to think about what they have read.

Usually, however, you are asking them to do something they don't want to do. They're lazy. They don't want to write for further information, they don't want to fill out application blanks, they don't like to cut out coupons, and they hate to lick stamps and seal envelopes.

The easier you make it for your direct mail audience to respond, the more will respond. Cater to their lazy bones. Always include a business-reply card or envelope. You will only pay for "live returns." Many a good intention has been lost while the prospect was looking for a stamp. Don't ask for too much information on a coupon. Checking boxes is simpler than writing a short essay.

One popular direct mail device consists of a letter and reply card combination in which the recipient's name and address are printed on a detachable reply card and mailed in a window envelope. The recipient need only tear off the card and put it in a mailbox. A mailing of this kind was used successfully as a preliminary announcement to teachers interested in summer session work. We can assume that these prospects were able to sign their own names, yet the mailing in which this was already taken care of for them far outdrew a similar mailing where they were asked to write their names and addresses. An added bonus: There was no illegible handwriting to decipher.

An old saying in the direct mail business is, "No piece is any better than its mailing list." This is especially true for promotional publications since almost all of them are distributed by mail. And the greatest percentage of the millions of pieces mailed are what could be called "unasked-for mail." Most people who find a publication in their mailbox did not request information or answer an advertisement; they are at best a neutral audience. Some will throw it away. Others may find it interesting, but will take no action. A few will read it, be interested, and take action. They will phone, write, come in person, and eventually register for courses, donate money, buy football tickets, and so on. The number of people in this last group determines the effectiveness of the entire mailing program.

Write a letter

Letters are probably the most used and abused form of direct mail. Many years before anyone ever heard of "junk mail," Henry David Thoreau wrote, "I never received more than one or two letters in my life that were worth the postage." Sometimes we may think that almost all of the folks who receive our fund appeal letters are kindred spirits with Thoreau.

Letters can be the most costly way of communicating with a public. It has been estimated that the average business letter costs more than $5.50 when you include the time spent writing and producing it. Yet with all of its obvious drawbacks for reaching a mass audience, nothing gets results like a good letter. The well-thought-out personal letter, carefully conceived and carefully directed, is a better public relations and fund-raising tool than the most elaborate brochure. It is the only way to reach a select group of a dozen or so people. If the same letter is to be sent to more than a very few people, however, you should use one of the methods for reproducing letters in quantity.

For certain types of prestige mail, such as "personal" thank-you letters from the president, a word-processed letter is convenient. The result is indistinguishable from individually typed letters.

As for the effectiveness of computer-generated "personalized" letters, go slowly. Hard-sell magazine subscription services have used the name dropping and computer letter technique successfully for years. Your readers are too sophisticated to be wowed by a mechanically produced letter that drops in their name every other paragraph. Recently, college admissions offices have begun sending computerized personalized letters to prospective students. All other things being equal, the personalized mailing should pull better than a form letter.

Mailing your direct mail

Tests run by large direct mail operations, which must get responses or go out of business, showed that there is a difference in the pulling power of an envelope that is hand stamped and an envelope that is run through a metering machine. Some difference was also discovered in the pulling power of a form letter mailed first class compared to the same letter sent out by third-class mail. You will have to balance the increase in response against the increased cost.

To send a letter by third-class mail, it must be a form letter—that is, a printed letter that is not typed individually for one person but for many people—and you must be mailing a minimum of 200. This letter may have the person's name, address, and title, and a personal salutation. A third-class form letter may also have a facsimile signature at the bottom. If cleverly done with a signature dropped in in blue ink, a form letter may sometimes pass as a personally typed job.

When an office handles large numbers of publications and has extensive mailings, it may also use a commercial mailing house or letter shop. These concerns are specialists in all phases of addressing and mailing. In most instances, they will process your work much faster and at less cost than could be done by extra secretarial or part-time office help.

Sometimes it is advantageous to have a printer mail a publication directly from the plant, especially if its circulation is mostly out of town and the distribution is almost entirely by mail. If the alumni magazine has a large national circulation, the printer can affix labels to the magazine as part of the binding operation. This is common practice for commercial and trade magazines.

In mailing operations, every extra worker movement is chargeable. For example, inserting an application blank into a booklet before stuffing in an envelope costs more than putting the two items together and then stuffing. However, having the printer insert the application in the booklet mechanically saves money. These are small points, but a series of extra charges can soon jump the total cost of mailing an ordinary job. Extra-thick catalogs, special wrappers, gummed tabs, string ties, odd shapes—anything out of the ordinary adds to the hourly or piece rate for a job.

If you are planning a large mailing of folders or letters that will be mailed in envelopes, use standard-size envelopes. Many letter shops have automatic machinery with which they can process standard-size economically and efficiently. Envelopes of an unusual size or shape will cost more to buy, process, and mail.

Every college office involved with direct mail should keep an up-to-date file of current postal regulations. A small mistake can cost hundreds of dollars or even lose a campaign.

The results

Every college public relations, admissions, or publications office should have some facilities for answering day-to-day mail requests. This might be a part-time student working two or three days a week or a small department with three or four full-time people. Requests for catalogs and information about the institution should be processed as quickly and efficiently as possible. And it's important to keep track of these responses.

You should analyze every direct mail effort in terms of its objective. This should be as much a part of your direct mail program as selecting a mailing list. Measure performance against the objectives you carefully stated when you were planning your direct mail campaign.

Tabulate the percentage of response. Did it equal or exceed the percentage you had planned?

Did the money or other response produced by the mailing equal or exceed your target amount? If the mailing produced any commentary from the recipients, how much was favorable and how much was unfavorable? How do these numbers compare with the previous mailing to the same audience?

What is the cost of the direct mail promotion compared to other means of reaching the same audience?

Tips for better results

Getting the most from publications sent through the mail calls for constant scrutiny of costs and devotion to details. In no other area of publications management is attention to scheduling so important, for nothing is as worthless as an invitation received after an event is held. Consider, too, the possible waste of a well-conceived and produced piece that is mailed to an incorrect address or, even worse from a public relations standpoint, a personalized letter with the name misspelled.

Nevertheless, despite the headaches it may sometimes present, direct mail is a growing method of getting educational information quickly and economically to selected audiences. Here, briefly, are 10 ways you can improve the effectiveness of your direct mail operation.

1. Use the computer to maintain your mailing lists. These may range from a large, complex database for your institution's alumni file to a word-processed list for people interested in lectures on French literature.

2. Printed letters with personalized salutations *can* be mailed at third-class non-profit bulk rates.

3. Personalized letters generally outpull "Dear Alumnus" letters, but they very often double the production cost.

4. Always print "Address Correction Requested" on your publications in order to keep your list clean. It pays to update your list constantly.

5. If you haven't used or cleaned a list for a year, better scrap it. Chances are that more than 30 percent of the addresses will be incorrect.

6. Mailing is a fixed-cost operation. Unlike printing, unit costs stay nearly the same whether you mail 1,000 or 100,000 pieces. To save money, keep your lists trim.

7. The success of any direct mail operation rests upon three factors: copy, lists, and timing.

8. Proper timing is vital. Plan your mailings to allow enough time for the piece to reach your public and draw a response. Provide a minimum of three weeks between announcement and event.

9. Check the delivery speed and reliability of mailings by putting your home address and those of several of your colleagues on all your mailing lists.

10. Keep records of all mailings that solicit responses. Discard ideas that don't pull and retest those that do in a variety of situations.

With the day-to-day accessibility of accurate computerized records, it is possible to move from direct mail to carefully directed mail. The shotgun approach is no longer necessary, and it is certainly not economical. Meticulously organized files will enable any institution to target selective audiences. Success in direct mail can be achieved when you combine good copy, attention-grabbing graphics, a well-timed mailing, and carefully chosen prospects.

Chapter 9

Building an Annual Report

After carefully weighing the costs in both money and time, most colleges and universities today follow industry's example in using the printed annual report as a major public relations device. In an annual report the institution can present its accomplishments as well as its problems to a selected audience. The corporation sends its report to its stockholders; the university sends it to those people whose continued support it seeks: legislators, benefactors, alumni, and so on.

Some institutions, such as land-grant colleges and universities, are required by law to publish an annual report. Others have published them as a matter of course for decades. Any institution not yet producing an annual report should seriously consider this opportunity to reach a special and influential audience.

If you look at annual reports from various colleges and universities, you will discover three main approaches:

• Some institutions apparently request annual reports from all departments on campus and publish them almost verbatim. The resulting volume serves as a quasi-official record of the year's activities. Little effort is made to package this information in an attractive fashion. It is hard to believe that anyone not compelled to read these documents would ever make the effort.

• The second approach, while an improvement, demonstrates the same defect. The annual report editor digests the reports from all the departments, adds some photos and graphs, and wraps the package in a colorful cover. Each department gets its due, whether or not it accomplished anything noteworthy during the year. (A newspaper editor following this formula would have to include a news story on each of the 50 states in every issue.)

• The third type of annual report presents the highlights of the year and the major problems and challenges facing the institution. The copy is trimmed to 5,000 or 6,000 words and is often packaged in a 16- to 32-page booklet. The editor adopts a narrative form or perhaps puts the report in the actual words of the president. The editor hopes that the recipients will spend a few minutes going through the report and will be enticed by pictures, design, graphs, and headlines to read it. The static often comes from heads of the departments that didn't accomplish any of the year's highlights and consequently aren't mentioned.

Which type of report your institution publishes should depend on your determination of audience and purpose. If your purpose is to report to the faculty, you will produce the first or second type of report—that is, the English department gets the same amount of space as the chemistry department, and no one is left out. If you are going to publish the annual report in quantity and mail it to busy people, you had better risk some faculty discontent and concentrate on the big issues.

Finally, another kind of annual report that is becoming popular for smaller institutions combines a review of the year's highlights with a summary of the year's fund-raising efforts. This hybrid is often published as a 32-page brochure—16 pages reviewing the year and 16 pages listing all contributors to the college. Copies are sent to everyone whose name appears in the honor roll of contributors. In contrast, a large university may send out a 64-page report covering only annual fund contributors. These reports are often timed to reach alumni just before their class reunions.

Once you have decided that you will put out an annual report, your first step in planning is to develop a concept of the piece. Before you determine any physical or editorial characteristics, you should answer these questions:

- What is the objective of this report?
- Who is my primary audience?
- What are my budget limitations?

Determining the objective

The objective of your annual report may be determined in part by the type of institution the report represents. A small church-related college may be obligated to report annually to the supervising church body. A state university may need to aim its report at the members of the legislature from which its fiscal blessings flow. A number of institutions now make the annual report a part of their development program; with others it tends to be a detailed financial report to the trustees.

The aims of the annual report should represent the policies and decisions of the top administration of the institution. Since most annual reports are signed by the president of the institution (in fact, many are called "President's Report"), the office assigned to produce the report should not have to guess what's on the president's mind. A half-hour conference with the president in the beginning can save many hours of rewriting and many dollars in production changes later.

Probably no college or university publication suffers as much from "committee-itis" as the annual report. Since the usual report sums up the activities and achievements of many departments and persons, the copy is often sent to those concerned for a "going over." This well-meaning action usually leads only to editorial chaos. Presented with a sheaf of typescript, almost everyone will turn editor with a vengeance. If you accept the changes, additions, and deletions suggested, you lose any hope of editorial continuity and style. On the other hand, if you ignore the blue penciling of your colleagues, you will find yourself in an untenable public relations spot—and you asked for it.

If at all possible, one person should gather together and write the copy for the annual report, and one person or office should edit it. Many parts of the final copy need to be checked with a variety of people, but ask them to check only specific items. The business office, for example, must provide and verify financial information, but the decision as to how much goes into the annual report and in what form is an editorial responsibility.

Determining your audience

Deciding for whom you are writing before you start writing may seem like the simplest of rules, and yet it is ignored consistently in annual report production. Often because the target audience of the report has not been clearly defined, the copy is written with one audience in mind, photos are selected for another, and the design combines the two in a package that makes sense only to the designer.

If your annual report is successful in communicating with one selected public, it will also do a good job of reaching a wide range of additional publics. As you begin to write the report, fix the members of your primary audience firmly in mind, and then tell them the things you want them to know about your institution.

While almost all corporate reports are produced in an 8½ by 11 format, college annual reports come in a variety of sizes. We have at hand a well-written, four-page, newsletter-style annual report that folds to fit a standard no. 10 envelope. At the bottom of a large stack of annual reports is a chunky 80-page, 9 by 12 piece printed on almost a pound of fine enamel paper. Something between the two is the best answer for most institutions.

A report that looks too flimsy and expendable will not attract thorough reading and is apt to hit the wastebasket rather than the reading table. An immense book that exhibits a lack of editorial and artistic restraint overwhelms the reader and often creates a negative impression of how the institution spends its resources.

How much *should* you spend?

Since annual reports can run the gamut from meager folders to weighty tomes, you should get a budget commitment early in your planning so you will know what the limits are. This should not be determined by how much a rival college spends on its report, but rather on an objective appraisal of how much you have to say and how important it is that your audience hear it. Most institutions have exciting years and dull ones. Capital fund campaigns, important anniversaries, or announcements of new academic goals certainly call for increased outlays, while a year in which it was "business as usual" may suggest a more modest effort.

In working up a budget, remember to include design, layout, photography, artwork, and graphics as well as printing costs. And if you plan to include a detailed financial statement or to put in figures at the last minute, allow an additional 10 percent to cover author's alterations. The minimum cost for the annual report of a small business corporation has been estimated at $6.50 a copy for 10,000 copies or less. In our experience, a reasonable starting point for most colleges and universities would be at least $2 a copy if *all* expenses are added up.

Planning a schedule

Now you have your objective, your audience, and your budget, when should you start putting your annual report together? You could begin as much as a year before publication, because much of the material that goes into a comprehensive annual report needs to be collected all through the year. Important campus events, for example, must be photographed as they occur, not only for the press but with the annual report in mind as well. It's a good idea to build a file of press releases and news stories that may be of use in writing the report.

Although you can do valuable advance work during the year, the actual production time of the report will usually be squeezed into as short a time as possible after the end of the institution's fiscal year. Following is a suggested annual report planning schedule:

Concept: minimum working time—four weeks. Schedule first idea sessions at least four months before your publication date.

• Meet with the president and other key administrative people to determine central theme and primary purpose of report.

• Decide generally what material must go into the report and in what proportion.

• Outline objectives and audience.

• Assign editorial responsibility and deadlines for rough copy. Most college annual reports are pulled together from material taken from reports submitted by deans and department heads.

Writing and editing: minimum working time—five to six weeks.

• Prepare a detailed subject outline.

• Working from all possible information sources, put together a rough copy draft.

• Drastically edit rough copy to eliminate repetition and items of lesser importance and to resolve conflicting statements.

• Arrange copy into major topics of interest.

• Rewrite copy for final editing, and verify all facts and figures.

• Write introduction and prepare editorial suggestion list for photography and art.

Layout and design: minimum working time—three to four weeks.

• Create rough layout and typographical specifications.

• Assemble photographs from files; arrange for necessary new shots.

• Gather data for charts, graphs, and illustrations.

• After approval of rough layout or thumbnail sketches, prepare comprehensive layout showing exact position of text, art, and photographs.

• Select a printer and consult with him or her on ink, paper, and special techniques.

Printing and distribution: minimum working time—three to four weeks.

• Set type. Galleys should be carefully proofread and checked with the people who supplied data and basic report information.

• Complete page dummy or a mechanical layout for the printer. This is the last point at which an annual report should be altered. Get a final OK from the president or a delegated assistant before the job goes to press.

• To save time and to ensure that the annual report looks exactly as planned, check press sheets at the printer's.

• Order envelopes and labels and affix labels to envelopes before the final printing of the report.

• Arrange for advance delivery of a limited number of copies for the president, administration, and board of trustees.

• Send copies to a selected list of donors, alumni, town officials, and so on, with the president's personal card, a personalized letter, or a hanger slip.

The minimum times for each of these production steps represent an ideal situation. We are personally acquainted with one annual report that was knocked out in 12 working days from copy to finished book. Avoid the overnight job at all cost if you can, for not only will it strain your relations with designer and printer, but rushing is bound to affect the quality and accuracy of the report. On the other hand, you should make every reasonable effort to get the annual report out as soon as possible after the close of the year the annual report covers. Certainly the receipt of a 1990 annual report in the summer of 1991 will not impress the reader with the institution's efficiency.

A financial report

In addition to an annual report, many institutions also put out a financial report. Like a corporate financial statement, the financial report has but one purpose and that is to clearly show the fiscal conditions of the reporting organization. While few college financial reports are circulated widely, an effort should be made to clarify rather than confuse in the presentation of fiscal facts.

A complete financial report should contain the following items:

• a short narrative review of the year's financial highlights, major expenditures, gifts, investments, construction, and so on;

• consolidated balance sheet (presenting a detailed breakdown of assets and liabilities as well as comparative columns for the current and past year);

• statement of current income, expenses, and appropriations;

• a summary of changes in funds; and

• accountant's opinion—reprinted as submitted if technically possible.

Using simple graphs and charts will help the readers interpret the various statements. Nothing has taken the place of the simple pie chart when you want to show where the money came from and how it was spent. A second color can be a great aid in putting together effective financial graphics.

One word about ensuring the accuracy of the figures in the financial report: Let the accountants have the final look. Even an experienced professional proofreader may not catch an error in a column of balance sheet figures. Accountants and fiscal officers are trained to find weak spots in a report. Let them have the last look before the proofs go back to the printer.

Using your annual report

An annual report is not a shotgun publication. You will want to pay careful attention to mailing lists. These lists should include the institution's chief benefactors, some if not all alumni, the faculty, the board of trustees, foundations, corporations that have provided support, large employers of your graduates, newspapers and magazines, selected townspeople, other colleges and universities, and libraries. Public colleges and universities will send reports to legislators, the governor, and political leaders.

Others might also put your report to good use. If your institution is in a small town, why not send copies to all barber and beauty shops as well as doctors' and dentists' offices? After a few months, they'll be well thumbed by these captive audiences. What about your own reception rooms around campus? You may also want to send copies to university clubs, high schools, fraternities and sororities, campus pastors, and perhaps even the State Department for distribution to foreign embassies.

A well-executed annual report is the single document that sums up the educational, research, and extension highlights at your institution. To get the greatest mileage out of it as a public relations tool, you should continually think about ways to extend its audience and usefulness.

If, for example, you are now printing 10,000 copies, the cost of an additional two or three thousand copies should not strain your budget and may prove to be an economical way to reach many previously overlooked groups. For instance, are you sending an annual report to all new and prospective staff and faculty members? Are copies given to visitors or made available to groups meeting on your campus? Does your admissions office have a supply for high school guidance counselors and parents of prospective students?

The annual report is a report to the public, and if it does its job well, it should create a positive impression with many different audiences. If you feel your annual report is great for prospective donors, but you wouldn't want the parents of a prospective student to see it, better take a hard look at it. The best way for a college to cut its public relations throat is to start saying different things to different people.

As a publication, your annual report is perhaps the most important single piece you produce. It also ranks high among all the ways in which your institution communicates with the public. It should not, however, be conceived and produced as a special project standing alone and different from the other informational materials you publish. A good annual report should fit into the institution's total publications program.

No matter how elaborate or simple your annual report, it should be an honest reporting of the facts as they are, not as you might wish they were.

Chapter 10

Handbooks

olleges as well as corporations have come to rely on printed handbooks to communicate necessary information to their staffs. For the price of a few score or a few hundred letters, information can be collected and published in an attractive handbook that answers most questions more completely than any letter can.

In this chapter we discuss four types of handbooks found on the college or university campus: handbooks for faculty, for service and clerical staff, for students, and for their parents. Some institutions combine the first two categories under one cover; however, many find that the interests of support staff are better served by preparing a separate, shorter handbook.

The faculty handbook

The typical faculty handbook is written with three reading publics in mind: prospective staff members, new staff members, and old-timers.

Negotiations for employment on a college or university faculty may span the continent. For example, suppose you work for a university in New York that wants to hire a professor in a California college. As negotiations begin, you airmail the faculty handbook to the applicant. The professor visits the campus for interviews, but she cannot possibly absorb all the information about the institution, the community, policies and regulations, and the like in personal conversation. When she returns home, she can look up items of particular interest in the handbook and share it with her husband and family.

If this professor, who is considering your institution among many, finds satisfactory answers to her questions in the handbook and decides to come to your campus, you can feel that the handbook is worth your time and trouble.

The comprehensive faculty handbook provides honest answers to almost any question a newcomer might ask. It includes a table of contents and a full index with cross-references. Larger colleges and universities probably publish a new edition of their faculty handbook every year.

The faculty handbook describes fringe benefits of employment: group insurance, retirement plans, hospital and surgical coverage, Social Security, vacations, and sabbatical leaves. Competing with industrial employers, the university must toot its own horn in the matter of fringe benefits, because its salary scale will probably be lower than industry can offer. Many colleges and universities can offer vacations, TIAA-CREF and other pension plans, sabbaticals, and cultural and educational benefits that industry cannot match.

The handbook also spells out policies on tenure, political activities, travel, patent rights, sick leave, academic freedom, contracts, outside employment, and the like. It helps the novice classroom instructor by explaining how to arrange a field trip, how to handle dropouts, how to report absences or disciplinary problems, and how to file grade reports.

A little research by the handbook editor can save hundreds of hours for the newcomer to the campus and the community. For example, the handbook can explain how to get new automobile license plates, how to register to vote, what state and local taxes to expect, where a family can picnic. The new faculty member and his or her family will want to know about schools, churches, libraries, museums, and other cultural facilities of the community.

Some few faculty handbooks try the "hard-sell" approach. For example, one small college boasted of "congenial co-workers of all ages, pleasant offices combining dignity and friendliness, a five-day week with no Saturday classes." It even included a salary scale for faculty. Most editors use simple and honest statements rather than superlatives, value judgments, and flowery phrasing.

To collect all this material is no mean task, but fortunately you need not do it every year. The handbook can usually be updated with a minimum of trouble. Faculty benefits, regulations, and policies do not change much from year to year.

Most colleges and universities sponsor an orientation for new faculty and their spouses, and the handbook can serve as a useful text. The president, business manager, and a dean or two deliver words of welcome and some comments on financial matters. After a couple of hours of talks, the program concludes with punch and cookies. Without some printed material such as a faculty handbook, participants may remember very little from the session.

The handbook can communicate far more information and in a form the newcomer can refer to time and again. Some institutions use the handbook as the basis for a more extensive orientation program. These programs cover several sessions and also include campus tours, visits to laboratories and libraries, and discussions by deans of other institutional areas. Each session deals with one section of the handbook, which the newcomers are asked to read ahead of time. At the session, they can ask questions about what they have read. These questions in turn can be helpful when the institution is revising the handbook.

Finally, the faculty handbook can be useful even to veteran professors who have been on campus for 20 or 30 years. During that time many changes have taken place. Absorbed in their teaching or research, they may know less of their institution than they realize. Most institutions maintain official codes or bylaws, but complete and up-to-date copies are seldom readily available to the average staff member. One large university publishes 4,000 copies of the faculty handbook every year but only 150 copies of the official code, which is usually about two years out of date.

If the handbook is designed to meet the needs of these three groups—prospective instructors, new staff, and veterans—the institution needs to print about half again as many handbooks as it has full-time staff. Departments will soon get into the habit of enclosing a handbook with every application sent to a prospective staff member. Deans and department heads will mark certain pages to answer specific questions.

The institution inaugurating a faculty handbook will discover after two or three years that the handbook has become one publication it would not want to do without. If it seriously wishes to hold its own with industry and other institutions competing for new blood, to conserve the time and prevent the avoidable frustrations of new employees by answering questions in advance, and to provide an accessible reference book for faculty members who have been on campus for some time, a college or university must consider the advisability of publishing a comprehensive and up-to-date faculty handbook.

The service and clerical employees handbook

The handbook for service and clerical employees need not be nearly as extensive as the faculty handbook. For one thing, most of the new employees in this area live in the community or are married to students. They do not need the introduction to the community that new instructors and their families welcome, and their needs are not as extensive. They are not worried about classroom procedures, research policies, sabbaticals, patents, how to submit grade reports, and the like.

A handbook for nonteaching staff covers such items as payroll procedures, vacations, retirement benefits, working hours, holidays, in-service training programs, taxes, overtime, sick leave, intramural transfers, personnel testing, first aid, group insurance, cultural opportunities, garnishment, credit unions, grievances, eating facilities, athletic events, civil service, and promotions.

This publication should be written in simple, straightforward language. The extra expense of cartoons and even a second color may be justified if it encourages employees to read the booklet. The personnel office can give a handbook to each applicant and arrange for distribution to those already on the staff. In the absence of major changes, you can probably use the same booklet for two or three years.

The student handbook

The student handbook may or may not fall under the province of the editor or publications director. Depending on campus tradition, this handbook may be the baby of the editor, the dean of students, the registrar, a student organization, or a committee of students and staff members. In most cases the college or university pays the printing bill.

Whoever is responsible for putting out the handbook can perform a real service to the campus and can further the public relations objectives of the institution as well. The handbook can become the campus bible for freshmen as well as upperclassmen. It may be the only place where students can find official regulations stated in readable prose.

As with admissions literature, the student handbook should be a combination of things students *want* to know and things they *must* know. Surveys of student opinion are useful to determine students' questions, but there is also a hard core of vital information that must be made available.

Here are some of the elements found in a random sampling of student handbooks:

- regulations;
- a message of welcome from the president;
- the academic calendar;
- athletic schedules;
- an introductory statement about the institution;
- activities and organizations
- school songs and cheers;
- administrative officers;
- convocations and lectures scheduled;
- housing units;
- study tips; and
- religious activities.

A few student handbooks are too ambitious and include career material and even class schedules as well as the basics listed above. Some refer students to other readily available publications.

Most student handbooks are illustrated with photographs, cartoons, or sketches. Some use two or more colors. The largest format seems to be 6 by 9, while other handbooks have been produced in a pocket-size format to make them easier to carry around. Some handbooks display the efforts of amateur artists; perhaps someone on the committee or a friend of the student editor "likes to draw" and was given the opportunity to try it out on the handbook. Unfortunately, the effect is often corny and primitive.

The language in a few of the student handbooks we surveyed was too precious for words. Copy for the student handbook need not strive for the dignity and legality of the university code or the official catalog; it should be informal, but it need not be banal, sentimental, ungrammatical, and gushy as well. It should certainly come up to the standards of English composition that the institution expects of its own freshmen. Regardless of who is responsible for the publication, it may be necessary for someone in the publications office to edit the copy. If the institution pays the printing costs and allows its name to appear on the cover, it must insist that the publication at least come up to minimum standards.

Some institutions mail the handbooks to new students before fall orientation.

If you plan to do this, you may need to print twice as many copies for the freshmen as enrollment numbers would indicate because only a handful will remember to bring the handbook to campus. Likewise, if admissions counselors plan to use the student handbook in recruitment, you'll have to increase the press run.

Ordinarily the handbook will be reprinted each year. This does not mean that it needs to be reorganized and rewritten each year. The type can be held and the corrections made with considerable saving of time and effort. A complete remodeling can be undertaken every four or five years at the most.

Student handbook editors will probably want to redo the entire handbook each year just as they redo the college yearbook. They sometimes feel that they have not carried out their assignment unless they start from scratch. While redoing the handbook may provide the student editors with valuable journalism experience, it rarely improves the handbook. The formula for a good handbook is not so easily arrived at that it can be reworked every year.

Deadlines are always a problem with student editors. More than once a professional editor has received a box of assorted photos and handwritten or typewritten stories with a note from the student editor that he or she could not get to it before the end of the school year and is now in (1) Europe, (2) ROTC summer camp, (3) the Canadian woods, (4) the hospital, or (5) a summer job that consumes every waking moment. The college editor has no choice but to put it together as quickly as possible to meet a midsummer or early fall delivery.

Gentle efforts to hurry the copy preparation along during the semester may meet with plaintive expressions such as "I'm getting behind in my studies" or "I have to cram for an important exam—sorry." Since the student editor and staff attend your institution to get an education, you can hardly tell them to put the textbooks aside and get back to the typewriter. You may take the opportunity to lecture the students on the meaning of responsibility, but in the end they can always insist that their studies come first.

From these remarks, you may conclude that we are cool toward the idea of student handbook editors. We are. Most of the outstanding student handbooks are professionally edited, illustrated, and produced, even though ideas and articles may be contributed by students. Cooperative sessions between the publications specialists and student leaders are helpful, but the ultimate responsibility falls on the shoulders of the college administrator. If any particular student contributor fails to meet a deadline, the editor has to step in and get the job done in a manner that will be a credit to the institution.

Some institutions don't publish a student handbook but instead spread the information it would contain among several other publications. There may be separate handbooks about the library, religious activities, information for foreign students, how to study, social etiquette and campus practices, sports, residence hall living, and fraternity and sorority life.

Parents are important too

Some publications directors make the mistake of ignoring an important constituency with a built-in interest in the institution: the parents of undergraduates. If anyone should be kept informed, it is the parents. They probably played a major role in selecting the college for their son or daughter; they visit the campus regularly, pay many of the bills.

Some colleges and universities publish quarterly newsletters for parents or put them on the mailing list for the alumni tabloid or magazine during the years their children are enrolled. Others publish an annual parents handbook that provides an orientation similar to that given freshmen. Some institutions send handbooks to parents of all freshmen. Some add the parents of all students admitted but not yet enrolled. A few send an annual handbook to parents of all undergraduates.

A parents handbook usually includes information such as the following:
- an academic calendar;
- descriptions of various counseling and health services;
- religious activities;
- major athletic schedules and how to get tickets;
- the institution's policy on alcohol and drugs;
- the grading system;
- the implications of scholastic probation;
- expenses and financial aid;
- insurance programs for students;
- housing options;
- checking accounts;
- policies on student automobiles;
- local hotels and motels;
- where to park on or near the campus;
- information on parents day or parents weekend;
- where to eat near campus; and
- a directory of academic advisers, college officers, and services for students.

With tight writing and editing, all this information can fit into a 32-page, 4 by 9 booklet.

Each of these handbooks, whether for faculty, staff, students, or parents, contributes to the efficiency and morale of the institution. Each handbook should be able to justify its existence and the costs involved in its preparation.

Chapter 11

Newsletters

M any colleges and universities have discovered that the regular newsletter provides a convenient and systematic format to reach a variety of reading publics.

Almost all of these newsletters have a standard four-page, 8 ½ by 11 format. Some use one color, some two. The makeup usually calls for two or three main stories on page one with possible jumps to other pages. Photos or other artwork may take up as much as 30 percent of the text space.

The many merits of newsletters

One use of the newsletter format is to inform alumni and friends about the progress of the institution. Although the college or university may publish an alumni magazine, it may send this only to paid-up members of the alumni association. The newsletter, published twice or four times a year, reaches all alumni and ex-students at a much lower cost. A typical issue might cover donations to the library, excerpts from recent campus lectures, new scholarships, additions to the faculty, a description of a graduate studies program, and brief items about campus events. Some colleges with limited budgets use a quarterly or bimonthly newsletter as their only regular communication to alumni.

Newsletters provide continuity

From the point of view of public relations and development, the newsletter provides the basic ingredient for a successful program—continuity. The alumnus or friend of the institution receives regular reports on programs and problems instead of out-of-the-blue appeals for funds. Through the newsletter the college or university develops a rapport with its supporters on which it can build when the time comes to ask for help.

Newsletters can also create or strengthen ties to parents of currently enrolled students. At least during the four years in which their son or daughter is enrolled, parents have a natural interest in campus activities. Too often their only communications from the institution are form letters from the dean, grade reports, and bills. The newsletter keeps them informed on a regular basis. Because many parents do not see area newspapers, newsletter articles can be culled from general college news releases.

Some institutions with radio and TV stations provide a monthly newsletter that includes a schedule of programs and describes program features. These mailings can grow to huge proportions, since there is seldom any charge to subscribers. Regular pruning of the mailing list can keep press runs and mailing costs within reasonable bounds.

A newsletter can be an inexpensive way to reach high school counselors, principals, and teachers. One example is *Purdue Reports,* now in its 40th year of publication. It brings information on new programs, admissions requirements, activities of interest to school people, etc., to some 7,500 readers in Indiana and surrounding states.

Beware of the GNP

The decision to issue a newsletter should not be made lightly. While it is usually easy to fill two or three issues, after the 10th issue or the 10th year of publication, you may have trouble finding worthwhile articles you haven't used before. Remember that a newsletter has value because of its continuity. A newsletter that invariably comes out late or often misses its regular publication schedule may reflect on the efficiency of your institution. And a newsletter full of chaff is not even worth publishing.

The advent of desktop publishing (DTP) in the late 1980s gave rise to a huge increase in the GNP (Gross Newsletter Proliferation). Departments have been known to purchase complete DTP systems to produce one or two newsletters a month. Quite apart from the question of whether the newsletter is needed and whether anyone will read it, the administrators who install the systems have probably not added up the total costs: the initial cost of the equipment and software, the annual maintenance contracts, the rapid depreciation, the time required for training, and so on.

We all assume a greater interest in our own departments and areas of work than outsiders will ever have. Some newsletters might be aborted in the planning stage if the originator asked, "Would I take the time to read this publication if I were not closely involved with the area myself?" Often the answer is "no." One of the authors receives at least 20 campus newsletters every month; he cannot afford to spend 10 or 15 minutes reading more than a handful.

Publications directors can perform a service to their institutions by counseling individuals on their campus who propose to start newsletters for their specialized areas. Many of these ventures are worthwhile, but others are sporadic efforts to communicate that die unlamented deaths after two or three issues. The editors soon realize that they really do not want to put out a monthly newsletter when the rewards of the research lab or classroom are so much more tangible. They lose interest or try to foist the editorship on someone else.

The publications director should make sure aspiring editors know how much time and effort go into a successful newsletter, and he or she should encourage them to consider other options before beginning a newsletter to which they are not willing to make a long-term commitment. They should realize, also, that a poor newsletter can create a negative image for their department or area, whereas the absence of a newsletter at least does no harm.

Chapter 12

Internal Communications

One of the serious problems facing American colleges and universities is the breakdown of communications within the institution. Institutions that once numbered staff members by the dozens now count them by the hundreds and those that numbered hundreds now number thousands.

Communicating with all these staff members—professors, researchers, extension specialists, administrators, and service and clerical workers—becomes a gigantic problem. Some of the channels of communication do not lie within the scope of this book. For example, the student daily or weekly newspaper should serve not only the students but the entire campus community. Memos, departmental meetings, personal letters, radio announcements, bulletin board notices, and posters are other ways to reach the campus publics.

Location is a factor

Beyond these media, many institutions find it desirable and necessary to publish an official house organ. To a great degree the location of the college or university determines the nature of this staff publication. The college that dominates a small town will issue an entirely different sort of publication than that produced by a metropolitan university.

In the small college town, the local daily may be willing to carry practically all the publicity releases furnished by the college information office. It will run stories not only about major changes and significant campus activities but even routine articles by English and history professors, attendance at professional meetings, speeches to Rotary clubs, promotions, and so on. A college-financed internal publication need not rehash this information since almost everyone on the staff subscribes to the newspaper and will read all the news they wish about their colleagues and the college.

The editor of the college house organ should concentrate on internal policy stories, discussions of various fringe benefits, and other material that the local paper will not use.

The editor of a university staff publication in a large city faces a different situation. The metropolitan newspaper will restrict its coverage to major events, programs, and staff changes. Even these may have to fight their way into the paper in the face of space limitations and competition from other educational news sources. The day-to-day activities on campus must go unreported, and the public information people know not to bother the city editor with routine news.

In a sense, however, the need for a well-written internal publication is more pressing in this situation than it is for the small college. Once the faculty members leave the campus in Big Town, they become anonymous faces in the crowd; their colleagues in the college town carry their identification with the college wherever they may go.

Professors in the metropolitan institution may live 40 miles or more from the campus. Once home after classes, they will probably not return to campus until the next day. They need to know that they belong to an academic community; that their university, although large and diversified, is interested in their welfare; that their colleagues are engaged in important work. The sophisticated internal publication can help build this esprit de corps.

Long lists of published papers, articles, and books can be a headache and a bore to the internal publication editor, but where these notices can claim no newspaper space, it may be worth it to include them in the staff publication. Professors are not above vanity, and they seek the approval of their colleagues and peers. A list lets the faculty know who is getting published and what is coming out of the institution that will help build its reputation beyond its classrooms. The lists can be printed in fairly small type—6 or 7 point—since no one is likely to read them straight through.

Avoiding the appearance of expense

The format of a college or university internal publication varies from typewritten pages to desktop publishing newsletters to elaborate two-color magazines, which rival *McCall's* in layout and photography. Editors encounter a universal faculty attitude when they begin to plan the internal publication. Many faculty members raise no objection to multimillion dollar building programs, landscaping projects, trips to European conferences, or the purchase of sophisticated scientific equipment, but their response to an expensive-looking internal publication is invariably, "Why isn't this money being used for salaries?" And the editor's rejoinder that the publication costs no more than pennies an issue per reader wins few converts.

The editor does well to accept this attitude and avoid antagonizing the academicians with what the layperson thinks is costly printing—glossy paper stock, fancy layouts, large photographs—even though these may actually be no more costly than some alternatives. The editor's goal should be to produce an attractive publication that does not look too expensive but that maintains the dignity and standards of the institution.

There is another danger in producing an expensive-looking magazine. In these days of austerity programs and economy drives, the administration may decide to save money by killing a luxurious-looking publication. Several fine internal newsletters and magazines have died such deaths in recent years. Perhaps had they stayed with one color, cheaper paper stock, and quieter layouts they might be continuing to serve as vital communication media on their campuses. Again, we should emphasize that the cost of the internal publication is not the determining factor but the layperson's *estimate* of the cost.

Frequency of publication ranges from weekly to quarterly. The weekly publications are often modest efforts. The quarterly publication may appear too infrequently to preserve continuity. The full-scale internal publication might serve its purpose better if it appeared every month or every two weeks during the academic year. The monthly cycle might call for eight issues, October to May. The summer months would provide opportunities to collect a backlog of feature articles to serve as a cushion for the rest of the year.

"One big happy family"

Just as some institutions publish separate handbooks for faculty members and for clerical and service staff, so do some issue separate newsletters for those two groups. Writing articles for a reading public composed of Ph.D.s and janitors may present a problem—even granting that some Ph.D.s show less intellectual curiosity and display less loyalty to the institution than some night watchmen and maintenance people do.

It is also unfortunately true that many people read no magazines and limit their attention to the sports and comics in the daily newspapers. To attempt to gear your publication to their interests invites frustration. Many institutions rely on student spouses as the bulk of their clerical staffs; these people may evidence only a mild interest in the institution itself and in their jobs. They are 8 to 5 people, and their main interest is in bringing home the paycheck. Miracles can happen, and a remarkable editor might be able to spark new interests in these people, but those of us who do not qualify as wonder workers might be more inclined to put our efforts in fields that would bear greater harvests.

Institutions that do not want to establish two different publications for the two groups may choose to aim the publication toward the faculty. If the other readers don't find these articles interesting, they can toss the magazine away. At least the editor will not have to adjust the contents and writing style to the lowest common denominator.

Is this an attack on the "one big happy family" theory of institutional life? Yes, it is. We do not believe this theory has much evidence to support it. When the head of the philosophy department and his wife invite the chemistry building custodian to play bridge, and when the nuclear engineering professor goes fishing with the new physical education instructor, we will reconsider the one big happy family idea. In reality, even the smallest institutions are highly stratified, and the interests of the various groups overlap only in small areas.

Ordinarily the competition from industry and rival universities is more intense for a statistics professor than for a building custodian or filing clerk. If the internal publication reminds the statistics professor of the advantages of working for your institution and furthering its goals, the time and expense involved in publishing the internal publication may be justified.

Planning content

A sampling of faculty/staff publications contained feature articles on the following topics:
- research in progress;
- personality stories about professors and administrators;
- picture features on people around campus;
- discussions of fringe benefits;
- official announcements;
- interviews; and
- roundup stories about academic departments.

Stories covered these subjects among others:
- staff credit unions;
- parking problems;
- the university press;
- enrollment trends;
- the financial picture;
- political responsibilities of staff members;
- faculty meetings;
- university club or staff social events;
- athletic opportunities for staff;
- sabbatical leaves;
- how medical insurance plans work;
- hidden pay;
- where to refer a prospective student;
- counseling agencies;
- convocations and lecture series;
- how to register for a course as a staff member;
- in-service training program for typists and secretaries;
- leaves of absence;
- college-community relations;
- United Way participation;
- a speakers' bureau;
- TIAA-CREF or other pension plans;
- building programs; and many others.

To research and write articles of this nature takes time. If you want to publish a house organ that is more than a collection of official announcements and publicity releases, you must be prepared to assign the necessary hours. A modest magazine could easily absorb 80 to 100 hours of work per issue for the combination editor-reporter-photographer responsible. Compared to this expenditure, the cost of printing could be secondary.

Material prepared for this publication can be recycled. You can rewrite many of these articles and send them out as news releases or use them in other publications such as the alumni magazine or a newsletter to high schools. You can file the photographs and use them again in the annual report, viewbook, or other appropriate publications.

Do not expect too much cooperation from the teaching staff in getting articles or suggestions or even letters to the editor. Rarely will a professor take the time to write an article for publication in the house organ knowing he or she will get neither scholarly prestige nor remuneration. Some professors will even deny that they read the internal publication, although readership surveys of the better publications indicate a rather high percentage of readers. The house organ is not ordinarily considered a prestige publication, and some professors will claim to ignore it along with *Time*, television, books written since 1880, and other manifestations of pop culture.

Furthermore, there is no use claiming that the internal publication is a free voice. It speaks for the administration, and everyone knows it. We can think of no house organ—corporate or educational—that consistently criticizes the administration. To expect an exception is to expect the impossible. Staff members are not so slow-witted that they will believe your publication to be a free and independent voice. For criticisms of the administration, readers should look to other sources—the student newspaper, AAUP newsletters, local newspapers, speakers at faculty meetings, and so on.

Distributing the internal publication

How should the campus newspaper or magazine be distributed? Some institutions simply send bulk orders to each department and ask the department head to have them put into individual mailboxes. Professors can pick them up at their office and read them at their desk or wherever they have a few spare minutes. Other institutions mail the faculty/staff publications to home addresses on the theory that otherwise the spouse and family of the employee won't get to read it. These institutions believe that it's more important to acquaint the professor's spouse with what is going on in the college than to inform the professor. Satisfied spouses who feel part of the campus community may mean more to a stabilized faculty than anything else. And dissatisfied mates who feel left out of things may be the reason for many job switches.

Before you decide on off-campus distribution, remember that an open circulation—in which the institution adds names to its mailing list regardless of financial costs or the importance of the recipient—can be very expensive.

Perhaps you should establish a flat policy of no off-campus distribution. Otherwise the institution may be compelled to set a subscription price to cover overhead, printing, mailing, handling, and so on. Extra copies can be available at the student union or faculty club for public distribution. Once you begin nonstaff circulation, you must face the problem of obsolete addresses and high postage and handling costs.

How much it costs to mail copies to the homes of staff members depends on the availability of up-to-date mailing lists. If such a roster is maintained by the president's office, secretary of the faculty, tabulating division, payroll office, or mailing service and can be used for a nominal sum, the cost of sending the copies by second-class mail will be small. The magazine or newspaper can be mailed without an envelope with the address imprinted on the outside back cover or on a label.

Calendars: What's happening

Even the institution that does not publish a regular faculty/staff periodical will probably issue a calendar of events. Every campus schedules a variety of lectures, plays, concerts, dances, debates, convocations, and athletic contests. A year's calendar will soon be inadequate as activities are added or dropped during the year. A weekly, biweekly, or monthly calendar informs faculty, students, and townspeople of what is happening on campus.

The institution can either print enough calendars for individual distribution to all employees, or it can print posters. If you print individual calendars, staff members can tack them up in their offices for future reference or take them home as a family guide to campus activities. Using posters, however, means that students as well as staff can consult the listings and that you will need to prepare fewer copies.

Whether you use a poster or a calendar, someone must take the responsibility of compiling the information. This may mean three or four hours of work for every issue. But certain ground rules must be laid down. The first should be that the sponsoring party is responsible for informing the calendar editor about the event in writing before a specified deadline: no letter—no listing. Trying to issue a calendar any other way invites chaos, endless arguments, and extra hours of work.

You must also determine what will appear in the calendar. Will the calendar list only events on campus? What about the staff-sponsored party in a private hall? Will the calendar list student activities and, if so, which ones? Should space be given to outside organizations that lease college facilities for their own meetings? Some of the rules may be arbitrary, but an arbitrary rule may be better than no rule.

Keeping control

Finally, the editor of the house organ and calendar will try to build confidence in his or her editorial judgment so that everyone above the editor will not insist on censorship privileges. An editor may decide to clear a delicate story now and then, but should resist efforts to set up chains of command involving several higher-ups who must read every word before publication. This can delay publication for weeks and months, run up alterations bills, and complicate life generally. If the administrators have no confidence in the editor or lose this confidence by seeing imprudent or inaccurate articles in the staff publication, they would be advised to let the editor seek employment elsewhere rather than to try to censor every word he or she writes.

Staff publications and calendars demand many hours of work. The planning, writing, editing, illustrating, and production of these publications can take up a professional journalist's full time during the academic year. The institution that takes a long-range view of faculty and staff recruitment, retention, and morale will see this as a wise investment of time and money.

Chapter 13

Special Purpose Publications

D uring the course of a year, a publications office may be called upon to handle a variety of printed pieces besides those major publications we have already discussed.

Campus maps and directories

Visitors and new students may find the campus map to be one of the handiest publications you can provide. It is also one of the least expensive publications to supply in large quantities for group distribution. When you order 20,000 copies or more, you can have an attractive map printed in two or possibly three colors for as little as 4 or 5 cents apiece.

The campus map can also include a capsule description of your institution; a rundown on libraries, museums, art galleries, and other buildings open to the public; a list of major offices; a summary of your areas of academic specialization; and so on. If your institution is located in a small city, you may wish to include a city street map showing approaches to the campus.

These maps can be distributed freely to students, visitors, conference enrollees, and townspeople. They can be available in racks in the student union building or at an information center. Some editors send copies to service stations in the area as well as taxi companies, bus depots, and airport terminals so they can be used to guide tourists and other newcomers to the area.

To produce good artwork for a campus map may take a skilled artist many weeks or even months, depending on the size of the campus, the number of colors used, and so on. To keep a map up-to-date on a growing campus takes additional time every year. Nevertheless, despite this cost, an attractive, complete campus map can be one of the institution's most useful publications.

Large institutions sometimes publish a walking tour map, which is useful for visitors who have only an hour or two to see your campus. This publication might take the visitor from the student union or the administration building to nearby points of interest.

Some institutions prepare an elaborate booklet especially for adult visitors to the campus. Printed materials designed for prospective students do not serve the same purpose. For example, taxpayers whose children do not attend the state university may want to know what they are getting for their tax dollars. A booklet that explains how the university serves the state in research, extension programs, adult education, ROTC training, cultural contributions, and the like performs a public relations job that an admissions booklet can never do.

In fact, admissions material that emphasizes the social, athletic, and extracurricular side of campus life may give the adult reader a negative impression of your institution. Whether seeking financial support or legislative support or both, an institution would always do well to tailor its material to its reading audience.

Floor plans and guidebooks

Campus visitors and newcomers can benefit from descriptive brochures for some of the important buildings on your campus, such as the student union, library, chapel, gymnasium, adult education center, and laboratories. A floor plan may be essential. A guidebook can indicate the location of checkrooms, restrooms, information centers, exhibit areas, and so on. These can be distributed from racks, counter tops, and in envelopes with conference programs.

Sometimes you can use the dedication booklet for a new building as a building guide. These booklets ordinarily include a description and floor plans. If you plan ahead, you can design them so that extra copies can be printed for this purpose; perhaps the dedication program could be printed on a separate sheet so that it does not date the booklet.

Speakers bureau directory

Some institutions help find campus speakers for outside groups such as service clubs, PTAs, churches, high schools, and civic and veterans organizations. The college may organize a speakers bureau through which all requests are channeled. A roster of available speakers may include pictures; biographical information; topics; a statement about the institution's responsibility in arranging programs; student presentations such as plays, concerts, debates, talks by foreign students; and a topical index.

Religion

Parents are often concerned about the religious opportunities at college, especially the facilities sponsored by their own denominations. They like to be assured that their children will be able to meet others of their faith and to receive spiritual counseling from clergy of their faith. A booklet describing the college's religious commitment (if it is a church-sponsored institution) or its attitude toward religion (if a state or private school) provides this information.

The institution should make it clear whether or not it requires Bible and religion courses, chapel attendance, or observance of any regulations against, say, drinking and smoking. For some prospective students this information will indicate the religious or spiritual commitment they are seeking, while for others it will suggest an uncongenial atmosphere. Even state and municipal universities offer credit courses in theology and lectures by prominent religious leaders. They recognize the work of a variety of student religious foundations and groups on the perimeter of the campus.

The booklet need not go into detail about the activities of the individual student foundations. A general statement on religious opportunities and a listing of the foundations should suffice; describing the full program of each foundation is better left to the individual organizations.

Financial aid

Financial aid is a subject of great interest to prospective as well as enrolled students. While the catalog and admissions literature contains statements on college costs and financial aid, many students need more than this. These students and their parents welcome a discussion of ways of working your way through college, the availability and average size of scholarships, how to apply for aid, the student loan program, part-time and summer job opportunities, and so on.

High school counselors as well as students and their parents value a frank examination of the costs of attending college today. Some institutions publish such unrealistic if not downright dishonest estimates of college costs as to do a real disservice to low- and middle-income families who must watch every penny to send their children to school. Institutions may quote a figure that includes minimum room and board and tuition but ignores other expenses such as books, transportation, clothing, laundry, toilet articles, haircuts, cosmetics, pizzas and soft drinks, entertainment, insurance, club dues, and contributions to church and charities.

Posters

No editor can avoid the task of preparing posters for campus events, graduate appointments, summer sessions, and so on. Many people consider these a bother. We Americans have never raised the poster to the art form that it is in Europe, although certain institutions, such as Brigham Young University, have set new standards for campus posters.

If you are preparing a poster, do not allow the client to forget that it *is* a poster and should not include information that will be sent to interested inquirers. A poster must often be read from two or three feet away, it may be high above eye level, it must compete for space with many other posters and so cannot be outsized. (Oversize posters are more likely to end up in the wastebasket than on the wall.) As long as the poster includes a clear statement on how to get further information, the fewer words the better. A pocket or a tear-off pad can hold return post cards.

Special announcements

Another large category of printing, which sometimes gets less attention than it deserves, is the short course or special program announcement. The sheer quantity of these often seems to preclude any attempt at quality. To issue 50 or 500 separate announcements over the course of a year—and have each be a superior job— demands originality, careful editing and proofreading, and many editorial and design hours. There is no way that they can be successfully "worked into" a busy publications schedule.

Many schools or departments within the institution fail to obtain adequate budget allotments to provide for a high-level series of announcements. The promoters pay honorariums for guest speakers, arrange banquets and tours, hire buses, and then, when the budget is almost exhausted, turn to the cheapest sort of printing for the direct mail announcement. It does not make sense to spend next to nothing for a "quick and dirty" announcement meant to persuade prospects to spend $200 to $350 for a workshop program. The prospect may well judge the quality of the program by the quality of the announcement—and respond accordingly.

Living arrangements

A helpful booklet discusses the pros and cons of different types of living arrangements at the institution: residence halls, fraternities and sororities, cooperatives, and private homes. This booklet should be sent to inquirers long before they have signed a contract or finalized their housing arrangement. Sometimes local circumstances make such a cooperative arrangement impossible, in which case the college-owned dormitories, the Greeks, and the co-ops issue their own separate booklets to try to woo students.

Minority recruitment

A fairly recent category of publications is directed to blacks or other minorities in an effort to boost enrollments from these groups. Some of these pieces include discussions of career opportunities for minorities in particular areas of study.

Foreign students

More than 366,000 students from other countries attend U.S. colleges and universities. Institutions with substantial numbers of foreign students may wish to publish an information booklet to prepare these students *before* they leave their homes. The booklet discusses what these students need to know, including passport information, travel costs, housing reservations, English language requirements, evidence of financial support, etc. It should be written carefully to avoid colloquialisms and ambiguities as much as possible. The foreign student may not have access to a native English speaker in his or her home. If you print these booklets on lightweight Bible paper, they can be sent airmail at a reasonable cost.

Programs for special events

Over the course of a year, you may be called upon to produce special programs for graduation, an inauguration, special lectures, and so forth. Because you will probably print only a limited quantity, you can usually afford a higher grade stock, deckle-edged paper, embossing, and other more costly treatments, which would be out of the question on other publications. Many of these events—and the programs for them—are traditional, and you would probably not alter the format or try anything new on these pieces.

Directories

Rather than include detailed information on faculty and staff in the catalog, some institutions publish an annual roster. The catalog listing for a professor might indicate only rank and highest earned degree. The roster would include all degrees as well as the institutions that granted them, the year the individual joined the staff, and so on. This roster may be of great value internally, but the information it contains would be of minimal interest off campus.

The publications office also usually coordinates the campus telephone directory. At one time this ranked as one of the most expensive publications because the institution furnished 3 by 5 cards for Linotype composition and then paid for the printing of the directory. Now many institutions provide the copy on magnetic tape and use a commercial firm that will provide free directories financed by the sale of ads. Class schedules and campus maps can also be produced at no or small cost to the institution by selling ads to local and national businesses.

Miscellaneous jobs

Pocket calendars have proved to be good public relations devices for colleges, alumni funds, and student organizations. Many people keep them all year long and refer to them often, if not daily. Each time they look at the calendar, they are reminded of the institution. You can also include important dates such as convocations, homecoming, and so on.

At freshman orientation, a few institutions hand out post cards depicting campus scenes—a low-key reminder to new students to "write home."

Some institutions provide notebooks for participants in on-campus conferences. Every other page is blank, but the printed pages have pictures of the institution or information about it. Since participants usually take this notebook home after the conference, the institution's message is also preserved.

A fact book about the institution may be useful to newspapers and radio-TV stations in the area. It can provide basic information such as when the institution was founded, its chief officers, areas of specialization, number of seats in the stadium, annual budget, and so on.

Tiny facts folders, perhaps 2 by 3 inches, are popular because they are inexpensive to print and easy to slip into no. 10 envelopes with letters.

No doubt in this chapter we have mentioned a number of publications that your institution will never need and have omitted others that your institution couldn't function without. This book is too short to discuss all the publications that colleges and universities put out: a financial report, a resource book for the media, an accessibility guide for handicapped students and visitors, summer sessions promotional materials, university regulations, etc., etc. The full scope of college and university publications is impossible to cover in a book, much less in a roundup chapter. But we hope we have suggested some publication possibilities that might fill a real need on your campus.

Chapter 14

Using Photos and Photographers

C ontrast is an essential quality in the making of a great photograph—or any work of art, for that matter. Contrast lends itself to description graphically more easily than it does with words. Even in its most complex combinations, anyone can understand most photographs (Margaret Bourke-White).

Imaginatively used photographs can turn a very ordinary publication into an effective marketing tool, an attention-commanding fund-raising piece, or a distinctive annual report. Almost everyone looks at the picture first, and even tedious technical material can be made more palatable when interspersed with photographs. Pictures are not, of course, the answer to all publications problems. A sprinkling of photographs through a dull and poorly organized college catalog is not going to turn it into a best-seller overnight. To paraphrase that much overworked Chinese philosopher, one poor picture is worse than a thousand poor words.

There are, however, many ways in which photographs can be used advantageously. While one really good photograph can tell an entire story by itself, pictures like this are rare indeed. More often, photographs supplement or illustrate the text of a publication. They can also be used as a feature of design or as graphic decoration to enliven the cover, title page, or sectional headings of a brochure or catalog.

Photos illustrate, supplement, explain

For the college editor, the primary function of photographs is to illustrate and supplement the informational material in the promotional viewbook, catalog, annual report, fund-raising brochure, or alumni magazine. The impact of a good photograph is unique. It can bring to life the ideas and personalities that make up the important story of your institution. A picture of the excavation and construction for the new library is much more meaningful than a paragraph of description.

Pictures with information captions can sometimes tell the story by themselves. For example, if a famous pianist visited your campus as part of your convocation series, which would tell the story more effectively—a paragraph about the event or a photograph of the pianist in concert before an appreciative college audience?

Ronald Parent, who was the editor of the award-winning *Notre Dame Magazine,* explained his philosophy of mixing copy and photography this way:

> We attempt to combine the written word with photography to enhance the importance of both. But our photographs and articles do not necessarily say the same thing. In fact, sometimes we deliberately use pictures to go beyond the copy. Photography isn't just a graphic device to make our magazine look nice. We want it to stand on its own—to make its own statement.

Careful selection and use of photographs can actually save you space and time in communicating with the public. You can use good photographs to emphasize major editorial points and help explain complicated technical matter. For example, let us say the purpose of the booklet about your alumni scholarship program is to encourage alumni to contribute to it. Along with the facts and figures, needs and goals, you could run some unposed pictures of students who have received alumni help. Realistic photos add a personal touch to any fund appeal.

Photographs can explain where words sometimes fail. Your chemistry department may be using a mass spectrometer to do important research. Perhaps a chemical corporation gave this equipment to your university. You would like to thank the corporation in your annual report and, at the same time, encourage similar gifts from other corporations. "Mass spectrometer" does not mean much to the average reader. However, an on-the-spot photograph of this apparatus actually in use makes your point in the time it takes a reader to scan a picture and read a caption.

Free-lance photographer Susie Fitzhugh makes the case for using mood-making photographs:

> Done correctly, a picture really *is* worth a thousand words. Not only can photography capture the look of a place or event, but it can also carry much more subtle messages. A photograph can evoke a mood, convey a feeling, and sometimes trigger an intensely powerful response. A message too emotional for words can nevertheless be spelled out gracefully in a photograph. And that kind of photograph has an honesty that can't be matched by a verbal description.

Photos as a design element: Cropping imaginatively

Don't overlook photographs as an important and economical element of design.

Using photographs in this way often means taking a fresh look at them. You can use a print in many ways in addition to the version in which you received it from the darkroom. Let's say you have an 8 by 10 print of your new dormitory at night. The activity and physical extent of the building are shown by many lighted windows against a dark background. You can use the print as it is to show the entire building, but you can also take a one- or two-inch side strip cut vertically from the photograph and run it next to a block of copy or a table of contents. Or you might try cutting the photo into thin horizontal strips, running copy lines between, and letting the "expanded" photo fill up an entire page.

If the photo didn't come out the way you hoped, and it's too late to take another shot, don't despair. Make it an editorial habit to scan every print for some portion with possibilities. You can sometimes use imaginative cropping to accomplish wonders with a cluttered photograph. Cropping a photo means that you mark off the part of the picture that you want to use. You usually do this with a blue or red china marking pencil by placing small lines on the border of the print indicating top and bottom and right and left limits within the original photo. By a stroke of crayon you can remove such unsightly elements as heating pipes, old light fixtures, filing cabinets, and even unpressed trousers and unshined shoes.

A handy tool for helping you visualize what may be usable within a photo is a set of two cardboard L-shaped frames. Mark off inches along the inside edges of each L, and you will also have a device for proportionally sizing photographs.

Since photos are hardly ever supplied in the sizes you intend to use in your printed piece, you should know at least one way to size or scale them to fit. For the simplest method, you need tissue paper, a T-square, and a triangle. Put tissue paper over the photo, and trace the squared-off sides of the entire print or the portion you intend to use. (Do this lightly enough so that you don't mark or scratch the photo itself.) Now draw a diagonal line (on the tissue paper only) from one corner of the traced outline to the opposite corner. To reduce the photo, you work inside the traced outline; to enlarge it, you extend the diagonal line outside of the original outline.

If you want to reduce a 10-inch wide photo so that it is five inches wide, measure five inches on the common base line and draw a perpendicular line up to the diagonal. The intersection of this vertical line and the diagonal marks the height of the reduced photo. To enlarge a photo, measure the enlarged width along the extended base line and draw a perpendicular to meet the extended diagonal. They will intersect at the height of the enlarged photo.

Slide rules and circular scales are also available to size photographs mathematically. You can buy these devices from art supply stores, or your printer may be happy to give you one. While they will supply you with quick, accurate dimensions for sizing photos, the less experienced editor may find it an advantage to see how small or large the photos will actually be in the final layout.

A word of warning on photographic prints—handle them with care. The printed halftone impressions you wind up with in a brochure can't be any better than the original photographs, so please don't fold, scratch, or roll them up. Keep them clean and flat in protective file folders. Two more don'ts—don't use paper clips to attach captions, and never write on the back of photographs, particularly not with a sharp, hard lead pencil. You need to be even more careful in storing, filing, and handling color slides and negatives. A minute scratch can ruin an irreplaceable slide. Treat your collection of prints and slides gently, and you will be able to use them over and over again many different ways, saving both time and money.

Treat photographers gently too

So far we have been talking about using the finished photo, and we have neglected the most important element, the person behind the camera. If you have a good photographer, treat him or her well, for that person can make an enormous contribution to the appearance of your publications. When searching for photographic services, make an extra effort to find the best professional talent available. The woods are full of eager amateurs and semipros who will shoot your pictures at reduced prices, but it may cost you more in the long run.

While they may not be counted on to fill regular assignments, student photographers are a good source for campus action shots and feature material. Let the student newspaper and yearbook editors know that you will pay for good prints or negatives. Going rates are $10 for published prints and up to $25 for unusually good exclusive photos.

In no area is the difference between a really competent professional and a run-of-the-mill photographer more pronounced than in illustrative photography. This is the kind of imaginative and lifelike photography used in national magazines and in the best college brochures, annual reports, and fund-raising materials. A top-notch photographer may charge as much as $800 to spend a day on your campus, while a local commercial photographer might only charge $150 to $300 for a day's work. Before you decide to keep the difference in your budget, consider what you'll actually get for your money.

An expert can produce as many as 50 good photos in one day of shooting and may often take more than 300 exposures. In three or four days, a keen-eyed and active illustrative photographer can provide you with an extensive file of campus scenes, students, classrooms, and laboratory photos. As the cost of the original photography is small compared with the overall expense of producing almost any brochure, it does not pay to settle for cut-rate photography.

Even after you find a satisfactory photographer, keep in mind that few, if any, professionals are equally good at all types of photography. Don't expect excellent portraits, news and sports shots, research photomicrography, projection slides, and graduating class pictures from the same person.

Don't expect your photographer to be a mind reader either. He or she needs to know the exact nature of the job, the purpose of the photographs, and how they will be used. It will save a lot of time if you make appointments in advance with the people the photographer may need to see during the day. In some cases a rough shooting script outlining the locations and actions to be covered will prove valuable. Make sure that you have secured clearances for shooting in classrooms, laboratories, and especially for contract research projects.

Once you have given precise instructions and cleared the way, stay out of the way. Resist the temptation to look over the photographer's shoulder. The photographer will appreciate it and get the work done faster and better.

Writing in June 1986 CURRENTS, Joshua Levine offered some sage do's and don'ts for improving photo assignments.

1. *Avoid posed photographs.* Nothing says "cliche" like four people with forced smiles squinting into a camera. No matter who the subjects are, they'll appear more relaxed if they look at each other rather than at some stranger with a Nikon. Your photographer should encourage subjects to talk to each other. Once they're distracted by their own conversation, the photographer can move around in order to capture the best composition and expression possible.

2. *Don't stage events.* If your photographer shoots an awards presentation or a fund-raising banquet, encourage him or her to take pictures of the event as it unfolds without stopping for posed pictures. If the photographer tries to be unobtrusive about picture taking, participants won't feel they have to play to the camera. The resulting photos should reveal more of the ceremony and less of the photographer's presence. Suggest that the photographer focus closely on faces to highlight expression and eliminate unwanted background.

3. *Try a new angle.* With a familiar subject, such as a person at a computer, get your photographer to take an unusual visual approach. To do this, the photographer may have to climb on top of a desk or lie down on the floor to get a readable image. A new perspective will at least make your readers pause to consider what they're seeing.

Building a photo file

What do you do when you need a picture for a rush publication and either bad weather or lack of a photographer keeps you from getting a new shot? The simplest solution would be to walk over to your filing cabinet and pull out a substitute from your photo file. This is not the answer to all picture needs, but a well-organized file of much-used campus photographic scenes can get you off the hook many times. No matter how many or how few photographs you use during a year, you should maintain a file of commonly called for subjects. This file should contain at the very minimum the following:

1. outdoor campus scenes including several views of each building;
2. indoor shots of a variety of classrooms and laboratories;
3. recent portraits of top administrative personnel and prominent faculty members;
4. student pictures covering a wide range of events and activities;
5. sports action shots of all varsity and intramural competition;
6. views of all public meeting rooms, auditoriums, field houses, etc.;
7. library study rooms, student unions, dormitory lounges, and cafeterias (all with students, please; don't keep *any* "no-life" photos in this category);

8. alumni activities, including head shots of prominent alumni; make sure you have a good collection of reunion and homecoming pictures;

9. concerts, lectures, and dramatic presentations; and

10. architectural and interior design details such as doorways, staircases, decorative windows; these make good illustrative spots to break up text.

Filling the gaps with stock photos

When your file runs dry and there's no time to shoot a picture, you may have to fall back on stock photos. Stock photographs are available from a number of sources and cover almost every conceivable subject and situation. Organizations that maintain extensive files of prints include trade organizations and business firms; professional associations; news services and newspapers; and libraries, both public and private.

Occasionally you will need a picture of a particular historical event, a technical laboratory shot, or a scenic view of your community or a nearby city. Stock photos may fill the bill in a variety of situations. They may often be obtained free of cost from industrial concerns or chambers of commerce. Libraries are a rich source of historical and specialized subject photographs, which can usually be borrowed for a low fee.

The neighborhood newspaper is a good place to turn for local background and news shots of events your publicity office couldn't cover. It's a good idea to have a regular working arrangement with the local papers so that they will supply you with prints of all photos they take of campus activities.

No matter from what source they are obtained or in what type of publication they are used, photographs can be a strong ally in putting across your editorial message. People tend to believe in photographs more than words.

Honesty is the best policy

The public's trust is an asset when you are using pictures to communicate an idea quickly and thoroughly, but it also poses a special responsibility for the editor. Be very careful that you do not present a false impression through the photos you select. No one expects your recruitment brochure to be illustrated with photos of unkempt students and decrepit buildings, but neither should it always include only the "best and brightest"—whether buildings or people. Make a selection of honest photos of real students in real classroom situations.

Nothing will get you in trouble faster than trying to fake "candid" shots. If you can't use honest photography to your advantage, the problems of your institution won't be helped by any kind of illustrative material.

But if you use photography with imagination and discretion, it can be the keystone of your successful publications program.

Chapter 15

Art and Design

I t is probably fair to say that the world of art has had little direct effect on college publications. Indirectly, however, the major art movements from Cubism to Surrealism to Abstract Expressionism have all had a profound influence upon the art directors, the designers, and the artists who set the tone for commercial graphic communication. And most college and university publications have in due time reflected these trends. However, the art we are discussing in this chapter is not just for museums and galleries. It can also have a valuable place in your institution's publications.

Like the term "copy," "art" has many different meanings throughout the graphic arts. This chapter deals with the creative artwork of commercial or fine artists as it is used in printing and publications. Artwork can be executed in a wide range of techniques—illustration, architectural rendering, etching, oil painting, charcoal and ink drawing, calligraphy, water color, cartooning—and it can be used effectively in a variety of ways.

Flexibility and control

One of the advantages of using art rather than photography is that the artist maintains complete flexibility and control over what to show and what to leave out. If your institution's most impressive building is an architectural gem that is hemmed in by utility poles and much less attractive buildings, it may be difficult or impossible to take a good photograph of it. But an artist can catch the flavor and character of the building with a few deft strokes and leave out all distracting elements. The artist's conception can also omit something else that dates a photo quickly—last year's style in clothes and cars.

Otto Storch, who was one of the country's most successful art directors and later launched a new career as a photographer, explained the difference between art and photography this way:

> There has been much said about the competition between photography and drawn illustrations. . . . It seems to me there is a need for both. The two, in many respects, are so different that they are hard to compare. *An illustration suggests, whereas a photograph is usually a statement.* The advantage in this to the illustrator is that he can get more reader participation by leaving more to the imagination of his audience.

A pen and ink drawing can be used in a variety of ways. Just changing the color ink in which it is printed produces a different effect. You might try reddish brown for a fall piece and a dark green for spring. A variety of effects can be obtained from one piece of art, which would not be possible with a photograph. A photograph would look artificial but a drawing can take on a new attractiveness.

Artwork can often be reproduced in varying sizes without losing any of its effectiveness. An interesting design effect can be created by using an illustration at its full size on the cover, reducing it to use as a secondary design element on the title page, and using it still smaller as a decorative paragraph break. Certain types of artwork provide flexibility in the production method you choose. A charcoal sketch, for example, can be reproduced as a halftone or a line engraving on smooth-coated or rough-textured paper.

When you are planning to use line drawings, you should strive for a relationship between the style of the artwork and the typography of the publication. For instance, a line drawing using bold black strokes and vigorous movement would combine very well with many contemporary sans-serif typefaces. A soft-toned, finely executed etching would be complemented by a facing page of one of the old style Roman faces.

Cartoons

Cartoons are probably the most poorly done form of artwork in college publications today. Most of the cartoons we've seen in viewbooks, catalogs, and student handbooks would be better left out. Readers of college publications are too sophisticated to accept anything that is artistically crude or lacking in humor and style. But don't dismiss the cartoon altogether. While we would urge you to beware of the amateur, cartoons, when done well, can put across an idea quickly. By injecting an element of humor, the skillful cartoon helps to fix an idea in the readers' minds.

Cartoons are particularly good when you have to explain rules and regulations as in a student handbook, for example. Here is a place where you can kid the red tape of the institution, make your point, and at the same time let the student enjoy it. Faculty and staff handbooks also lend themselves to cartoon treatment. Cartoons can be used to spell out personnel regulations, retirement benefits, vacations, food service, and many other aspects of staff and personnel policy.

Maps

Almost all institutions put out a campus map. It may be a simple layout of blocks, roads, and buildings, or an elaborate and professionally done rendering of the entire campus in perspective. Professionally executed perspective maps may cost from $20,000 to $50,000 just for the preliminary work and drawings needed to depict accurately a complex university campus.

You are in luck if you know an artist who can transform a flat outline map into a "three-dimensional" view of your campus. A map that shows the main architectural features of buildings and also gives the visitor and new student an idea of their actual size and exterior is much more valuable than a flat presentation showing just the location of the buildings. Adding a second color so that buildings appear in brick red or yellow against a contrasting background also improves the usefulness of the campus map.

A word of warning: Don't try to use part or all of an already printed map of your area. You may think that the city or state being mapped is in the public domain and, therefore, a map of it also belongs to the public. But most maps, even those given out at service stations or by chambers of commerce, are protected by copyright. Reproduction of any portion of these may put you and your artist at risk of legal action for violation of the copyright.

You can publish a campus map without cost to your institution. Commercial firms will publish a "free" campus map in exchange for selling advertising in the maps to cover their printing costs and make a profit. Many institutions have signed on for these services at considerable savings in time and money.

Seals and logos

All institutions have a seal, a coat of arms, or at least a monogram. Often this is a strange-looking device that was designed many years ago for forgotten purposes and for different publishing and printing conditions than exist today.

If you have to use an antique seal on official and historical documents, you can still have a bright new one designed for student and promotional materials. An eye-catching college seal can be used in a variety of ways. Printed small in the corner of your institution's stationery, it can be repeated over and over again and will become an identifying mark or trademark for your college or university. An attractive seal or logotype can serve as a focal point for a whole family of publications. Using the same graphic device throughout all of your publications can save you considerable time and money and at the same time ensure recognition for your catalogs or publications series.

Agreeing on the proper symbol to represent the institution may not be easy, as this story from a Florida newspaper shows:

> One of the most hotly debated issues at the University of Florida does
> not concern the football team's woes or the search for a new president.

It is over the selection of an official logo. "Any idiot that suggests either alligators, palm trees or football helmets should be shot," a member of the College of Medicine wrote to university administrators. "After all, we are an institute of academic learning and not an extension of the football team."

The search for a new logo has gone on for about two years. It began after a survey revealed that various academic departments were using a sundry collection of seals, insignias, and symbols.

The architectural rendering

The most expensive art that commonly appears in college printing is the architectural rendering. Hardly ever does a capital fund-raising brochure appear without at least one architect's rendering of a proposed building, laboratory facility, or student lounge. An architect's rendering is much more than an "artist's sketch"—an often fanciful interpretation of how the building *might* look. The architect's rendering is usually meticulously drawn from approved building plans. The completed structure should bear some resemblance to the architect's rendering. A single, expertly done architectural rendering of a major building may cost between $800 and $2,500. This is a specialty for which there is great demand, and the demand sets the price.

Using art to add interest

Contemporary art, or what succeeding generations will call "modern art," while sometimes unintelligible to the public, may lend itself to interesting publication use. You may find paintings done by members of your own art department that would make fascinating cover designs. In using this type of art, you do not look for pictorial representation, but rather for color, excitement, and eye-catching design. If your budget is severely limited, you may find that you can sometimes reproduce an oil painting effectively in black and white. It won't have the brilliance or the feeling of the original, but it may be worth a try. If you are reproducing an oil painting in one color, using a tinted stock or a linen-textured paper helps to catch the mood of the original.

You may find interesting design and art possibilities in the educational and research subjects of your institution. Fields such as astronomy, metallurgy, biology, geology, and chemistry offer many unusual patterns and designs that an artist could use to create original and striking effects.

The work of graphic artists, graphic designers, and art directors overlaps at many points in producing a publication. Add to their ranks the relatively newly arrived computer designer and the often forgotten typographer, and your choice of experts becomes even more complicated. If you can find a person who is truly competent in any one of these areas, he or she is sure to have a broad understanding of the whole field of graphics.

Count yourself fortunate if that expert also possesses the creative skills to set your publication apart from the mass of material sent out by most colleges and universities. While most graphic designers know the basic principles of legibility and readability, we have all seen examples of design that sabotages the message it is supposed to help convey: type printed over a busy background; extensive use of all caps, italics, and reverse type; black ink or varnish on black paper that forces the reader to manipulate the printed piece to decipher the title; yellow type on white stock; and so on. From time to time every editor or publications director will have to veto such design proposals rather than sacrifice the message.

DTP

Desktop publishing has revolutionized the approach to graphic design and type-setting. Until recently the Linotype machine, invented in 1885 by Ottmar Mergenthaler, ruled the typesetting roost. During that time changes in technology were few, but now they come on a monthly basis. So rapidly is this technology developing that we won't attempt to describe the state of the art in 1991 as we hope that this book will serve readers for some years to come.

Readers practicing graphic design in the 1990s are undoubtedly familiar with desktop publishing. They will find uses for such software as Adobe Illustrator, Aldus Freehand, MacDraw and Cricket Draw for the Macintosh and Versicad, Auto Cad, and Microsoft Paint Program if they use a PC.

We should not expect a word-processor to equip a mechanical engineer to compete in news and feature writing with someone who holds a degree in journalism and has logged years of editorial experience. Likewise, we should not assume that a Mac or PC and assorted software will turn an amateur into a graphic designer. So far no one has invented a machine that will substitute for talent, creativity, and taste.

Typography sets the academic tone for your printed material. Today most type is picked willy-nilly by poorly trained computer operators. Cost is certainly a factor—let's face it, a floppy disk is a lot cheaper than a designer.

Typographically speaking, a computer program gives you almost too many choices. You want 7½ point Italic Baskerville letter-spaced and flush right and left? You've got it.

Can excellent typography be produced by computer? Absolutely. Hermann Zapf, the foremost type designer of the 20th century, predicted the widespread use of computer typography some 25 years ago. Zapf, who successfully bridged the aesthetic gap between centuries-old calligraphy and modern technology, made these observations in a lecture at the Carnegie Institute of Technology:

> Obviously, typography-by-computer is bound to be more exact than the work of a human compositor. The automated machine can execute any and all functions of the compositor. Without fail, it performs according to the programmed information and instructions that are fed

into it. Putting in running heads, chapter headings and folios, captions and subtitles, picking out references and footnotes, while simultaneously eliminating "widows," short lines at the top of a page, hyphenations that break over a page and other typographical intricacies are all well within its capabilities. The computer literally thinks continually about the accuracy of the tasks it performs. With computers, no typographical business will ever have to find a good compositor to replace the man who is not working with necessary care. There will be no questions about whether or not in a large volume all lines with caps are spaced equally, or in complicated compositions whether all specifications and details have been observed. There will no longer be any anxiety about the compositor remembering all the designer's instructions and passing them along accurately to his colleague on the next shift.

A computer can be programmed for any requirement of composition—including hyphenation. Theoretically, the computer can produce perfect composition steadily, even when it is digesting complicated technical or scientific literature.

Computer graphics is also well-established as a viable art form. Starting a few years ago as image-forming games devised by imaginative computer programmers, computer graphics can generate corporate symbols as well as architectural plans. Recently the noted sports illustrator and muralist Leroy Niemann, using computer graphic imagery capabilities and a palette of more than 200 "electronic pigments," created a series of action paintings working only with a video screen and an electronic stylus. Your campus computing center may turn out to be the source of an arresting catalog cover.

Color

Introducing full-color artwork into your publications program calls for careful planning and even more careful budgeting. While still restricted by cost in college publications, four-color process printing is growing in use, particularly for covers of long-run brochures and in fund-raising materials.

Be careful when you are selecting art to reproduce in full color. All artwork does not reproduce equally well. Artists' colors are generally divided into four types: water, tempera, oil, and pastel. Water colors have transparent pigments while tempera, oil, and pastel colors are opaque. In painting with water colors, the artist applies thin layers to build up tones. The engraver's camera tends to see through these layers, so that covered up work or corrections will appear on the negative. Tempera pigments, however, are opaque and may be applied much more heavily. They usually provide good contrast and reproduce well.

Oil pigments are easy to reproduce. Corrections and overpainting can be done without difficulty and do not bother the camera, which picks up only the reflected light from the surface. Pastel colors also reproduce well.

Whether a simple line drawing or a full-color reproduction of an oil painting, the art that finally appears in your institution's publications must be more than just technically well-executed. It should honestly reflect the spirit and traditions of your institution. If yours is a traditionally oriented liberal arts college, you would not want to put the work of a Dadaist artist on your catalog cover. The kind of art you use should fall into place without clashing with the overall design scheme of your publications program. It should complement and strengthen the editorial message and be in character with both the institution and the cultural background of the readers.

No matter what kind of artwork you seek or how you intend to use it, sooner or later you have to deal with the artist. Your artist will probably not sport a beard, wear sandals, and live in a garret. These days it's tough to tell an artist from an accountant or a shoe salesman. In any event, do not mistake an offbeat lifestyle for artistic creativity. The successful commercial artist is usually a good businessperson and makes every effort to please customers as well as his or her aesthetic conscience.

Where do you find an artist? Begin by consulting someone who buys artwork regularly, such as an art director of an advertising agency or the production manager of a publicity firm. Even a small ad agency often has contacts with a number of commercial artists. Since artists specialize, the art director or production manager may keep a file of artists' styles and techniques such as illustration, cartooning, fashion, lettering, and layout. Since no artist does his or her best in every technique, it is important to match the artist to the graphic idea you have in mind.

Don't overlook the art department of your own institution, but do proceed with caution. A professor who gives a splendid lecture on art appreciation may not know a "rough" from a "comprehensive." However, it's worth a search; some of the nation's top graphic artists work on college campuses, and many of them have never been asked to do a job for their own institution.

Paying for it

How much does artwork cost? The answer could be anywhere from $25 for a single spot drawing by a beginning artist to $5,000 for a cover treatment by a nationally known illustrator. Most commercial artists set a minimum fee for any job no matter how small. Others will charge by the hour, including time spent for consultation as well as creative work. However the artwork is to be priced, the buyer and the artist should have a clear understanding of the job, the time it may take to complete, and an approximate total cost. If your budget is severely limited, let the artist know what you have to spend before becoming involved in a project that may prove embarrassing to you and painful to him or her.

In most cases, you should purchase the final artwork, free and clear for all types of reproduction. For instance, an intelligent and creative artist will put a good deal of careful planning into the sketch, engraving, watercolor, or oil painting. It will have a certain timelessness that will enable you to get your full money's worth by using it in a variety of ways.

Getting the most out of artwork in your publications calls for good judgment on your part and creativity and technical competence from the artist. If you have to settle for mediocre artwork, do without it.

Chapter 16

Stretching Your Publications Dollar

B   *e not the first by whom the new are tried*
     Nor yet the last to lay the old aside.
                                    Alexander Pope

No editor wants cheap publications, but everyone wants inexpensive ones. If cheap printing were the sole objective of a college or university publications program, we could simply advise black ink on newsprint as the standard of excellence.

Cheap publications may turn out to be the most expensive if they do not do the job they are supposed to do. In other words, you may not be able to *afford* cheap printing. If a particular publication fails to attract the quality of students, the funds, or the public support you need, it is no bargain at any price.

The college or university editor should conduct a continuing missionary program to convince campus colleagues that printed material bearing the name of the institution should not be looked upon as something ephemeral, dispensable, secondary. The appearance of the publications of your institution may carry just as much weight with your various publics as the architecture and landscaping on campus. The editor must fight the idea that printing is the first logical place to trim the institutional budget.

Meanwhile, the editor may have to use every trick of the printing trade to stretch the publications budget. Even after he or she has succeeded in establishing a positive climate for printing excellence, the editor must continue to devise ways and means to get more for the college's dollar.

Here are a number of ways in which experienced publications specialists save money without sacrificing essential quality:

1. Edit copy, not proof. One sure way to trim printing costs is to tighten editing and adopt a hard-line policy on alterations. If fiddling with copy in galley form is expensive, it is even more costly once the job has reached the blueline or press proof stage. An hour of typesetting may easily cost $40, and an idle press may cost several times this much. The more errors and style corrections you can catch before copy is typeset, the less your jobs will cost.

One-time editorial decisions can effect long-time savings. For example, a decision to limit catalog course descriptions to 35 words may save your institution thousands of dollars over a decade.

2. Plan. Printers who bid on short-delivery jobs tack on whatever they will need to cover possible overtime pay. On the other hand, by extending your production schedules, you will find quality printers who will offer low bids on your work if they can use it as fill-in between rush jobs. The quality need not suffer, but the printer will be able to use equipment and personnel to better advantage and can pass some of the savings along to your institution.

3. Avoid frills. In many situations, the use of odd sizes, blind embossing, fancy folds, four-color process, gold stamping, die-cutting, special scoring, and the like is a waste of money. Make sure decisions to choose these options are sound from the standpoint of readability, good design, and economics.

4. Shop for design. If your design is done on the outside, shop around. Creative design work that may be quoted at $80 to $100 an hour in New York and Chicago may cost half as much in a smaller city. Find young and eager designers who are building their portfolios and would like to include some samples from your institution. Perhaps art and design professors on your campus may do a good job on your publications, especially if they have production experience. The same holds true for faculty spouses with design training.

5. Pick typefaces with care. Favor typefaces that are large on the body; some 10 point faces are smaller in actual printed size than some 8 point faces such as Garamond. Choose faces with more characters per pica. In photocomposition, specify light-to-moderate kerning. (Kerning refers to the reduction of white space between letters.) By adjusting the kerning, you can preserve readability but cut the length of copy by 3 to 5 percent.

6. Get more characters per page. You can get more characters per page by changing the column measure. If you are setting a column 25 picas for a 6 by 9 book, you may wish to consider going to 28 or 29 picas. Even with smaller margins you will maintain readability with these measures and provide ample white space. Sometimes you can trim costs by going to a slightly larger page size with a double column format.

7. Do your own camera-ready pasteups. You will pay $30 to $40 an hour for pasteups in most print shops. Perhaps you can handle many of these jobs on campus. On one recent publication, a printer asked $380 to prepare keylines for a small booklet; a senior design student did the work for $40. (And if you use DTP, you can eliminate most of your pasteup costs altogether.)

8. Use self-mailers. Do you really need to use an envelope to get your publication to its destination? If you can get by with a self-mailer, you save the cost of an envelope and stuffing. Most of the magazines you subscribe to come through the mail without envelopes or wrappers; your catalog and other publications will get to the readers in about the same condition with or without an envelope.

9. Get bids on all but the smallest jobs. View the bidding process as a method of saving money rather than a bother. Perhaps small jobs under $500 or so may not be worth bidding out, but in most cases going through the bid process will save money.

Here are several guidelines for soliciting bids:

• Never ask a printer to bid if you would not give that firm the job if it has the lowest bid.

• Match your printing specifications with the vendor's equipment and personnel.

• Never limit yourself to vendors in a particular city or region if you can help it.

10. Insist on realistic press runs. Some departments never order enough copies of their publications, while others are hoarding theirs for the millennium. Here is a good use for a planning guide. Encourage the customer who originated the publication to work out a detailed distribution list before specifying the press run. The customer might begin with the idea that 5,000 makes a nice round press run and then realize that no more than 2,000 people in the Western Hemisphere would ever consider attending the symposium or enrolling in the new curriculum. On the other hand, he or she may discover that the distribution list actually calls for twice as many copies as first planned.

Point out the cost advantages of ordering an extra thousand copies at the time of the first press run, but do not talk the customer into ordering excessive quantities. While ordering an extra thousand copies brings down the unit cost of the job, they do cost money to print, to ship, and to store, and they also tempt the customer to indulge in indiscriminate mailings.

11. Consider setting type in-house. Savings may result from setting your own type by desktop publishing, but sometimes these savings evaporate when you consider *all* the costs.

Thomas A. Myers, director of communications for the development office at Western Michigan University, examined some of the pros and cons of desktop publishing at a recent West Michigan Electronic Publishing EXPO:

> • *Desktop publishing saves money.* False. (Unless you are one of those people who calculate the cost of operating an automobile solely on the off-the-lot purchase price.) If you are serious about doing professional publications, the rapid evolution of electronic publishing demands significant ongoing expenses for training and for hardware and software upgrades.
>
> • *Desktop publishing saves time.* False. Your time will be spent in different ways, but you probably will spend more time as an electronic publisher than you did as a traditional publisher. You are moving from a long-established method of producing publications to a rapidly evolving new way to accomplish the same end product, and you probably are assuming many new tasks, such as typesetting and keylining, that you previously had others perform. Just keeping up with the technology can be a full-time job.

• *Desktop publishing provides greater individual control over the publication process.* True. Using electronic publishing, the individual can control virtually the entire pre-press operation. Control is a tremendous benefit to the individual publisher and to the organization he or she serves. This is the best and really the only valid justification for the cost of desktop publishing.

12. Use lighter-weight paper. Paper, like tomatoes, is sold by the pound. If you can switch from a 50-pound sheet to a 45-pound sheet, you will save about 10 percent of the cost. Look at your paper requirements. If you can get by with a 60-pound sheet instead of a 70-pound sheet or with a 50-pound instead of a 60-pound, you will cut paper costs and perhaps postage costs as well.

Improvements in the strength and opacity of today's papers mean that a 45-pound sheet is no longer considered lightweight. By definition a lightweight sheet is between 17 and 35 pounds and includes the various Bible papers. You will pay a premium per pound on these lightweight papers but will probably come out ahead when all things, including postage, are considered.

13. Ask printers to suggest paper. Printers often buy paper in large quantities and can pass along some of the savings to their customers. Many house sheets have the same weight, opacity, and finish as the sheet you have specified but cost much less. You can sometimes get bargains in discontinued paper and closed-out stock. If a printer suggests an equivalent sheet, ask for a sample to make sure it will fit your requirements.

On some publications you may wish to go "first class," but remember that not one reader in a thousand can tell the difference between a No. 1 and a No. 3 enamel. Be sure you can justify using the premium grade, which only a paper salesman or experienced printer would recognize. One major university saved more than $6,000 a year by switching from a rag content stock to a No. 1 sulfite for its stationery; the publications director says no one has noticed the change of stock.

14. Stick with standard sizes. Such sizes as 8½ by 11, 6 by 9, 5½ by 8½, and 11 by 17 are cut from standard press sheets and eliminate waste trim. Why pay for paper that is never printed? Standard sizes also save money on presswork.

15. Take advantage of web presses. The web press prints from rolls instead of sheets of paper; paper bought in rolls may cost 30 to 40 percent less than paper that must be cut into sheets. Web presses also run faster than sheet-fed presses. Years ago web presses were considered only for jobs of 25,000 impressions or more, but now many printers own small webs that are well suited for jobs of 10,000 copies or fewer. Identify the printers in your area with web capabilities, and compare their bids with those of sheet-fed printers. Your savings will be greater if you design a 5½ by 8½ book rather than a 6 by 9 book, because the former size fits web specifications.

16. Solicit bids from printers with Cameron belt presses. About 15 Cameron belt presses have been built and are in operation in the United States, and a few others have been installed overseas. These presses print from a slightly raised surface using plastic plates affixed to a continuous belt; the process is closer to letterpress than to offset or gravure. In a sense the Cameron system combines the pressroom with the bindery since rolls of paper start at one end of the Cameron and perfect-bound books come out the other.

These presses print in units of 12 pages or varying amounts depending on the size of the book. The presses are best suited for books of 96 pages or more that do not have halftones or that can get by with halftones in coarse screens. The quality is not quite as good as sheet-fed offset, but the prices are attractive and the delivery is usually three to six weeks. As many as 200,000 impressions have been run from one set of plates. Smaller runs up to 200,000 impressions can then be stored for any possible reruns.

17. Choose cheaper bindery methods. Specify perfect binding instead of stitching or stapling. New adhesives keep the pages from falling out of a perfect-bound book, and perfect binding is usually less expensive than other methods. For some brochures, you can cut costs by using a foldout treatment instead of stapling.

18. Try a tabloid. For economy, nothing beats black ink on newsprint printed on a web press. If you can fit a publication into this format—class schedules, alumni newspaper, summer sessions announcement, or whatever—you may find substantial savings. Many small daily newspapers have purchased web offset presses and will give low bids for the work, which can be done on weekends or after the daily newspaper press run.

19. Let other people pay. More and more institutions are using ads to pay for their telephone directories, schedules of classes, football programs, maps, and so on. They either sell ads to local merchants or enter into an agreement with a publisher who will provide free copies in exchange for the use of the information provided by the college or university. Be sure to check the credit rating and reputation of any firm offering to provide you with free publications financed by ads. Some fly-by-night outfits have inflicted great public relations damage by their methods. Ask the firm to give you a list of recent clients, and check to see if these clients have been satisfied with the arrangements.

20. Go biennial instead of annual. Most colleges have reported slower growth or even a decline of students, faculty, new programs, and the like during the past few years. The need for annual editions of such publications as the catalog or faculty roster is not so great as it was a decade ago. Substantial savings in editorial costs, typesetting, and printing can be effected by going from annual to biennial editions. Besides the catalog, other candidates for the switch to biennial include the faculty handbook, campus map, and student handbook.

21. Use student help. Use your institution's students to write articles, edit copy, paste up, proofread, and do editorial research. They get practical experience and spending money, and you get an extra pair of hands. Many directors work through the journalism or art departments to find students who can contribute to the work of the publications office. Some offices make a standing offer to student photographers to bring in their contact sheets; the director selects photos he or she would like and pays so much per print. Sometimes you can even find a work-study student whose wages are paid 80 percent by the federal government.

22. Resist efforts to "dress up" publications. When some faculty people do not get the result they expected from a mailing, they assume it was the quality of the printed piece that was the culprit. It may not occur to them that their program has a limited appeal or that they were soliciting the wrong people or had established an unreasonable tuition. If the publication was in one color, they may want two, three, or more. More pictures may do the trick.

The editor must evaluate these recommendations and put the printed piece in its proper perspective. He or she is an editor, not a magician, and the publications office cannot be expected to accomplish sleight-of-hand tricks.

23. Study postal regulations. Postal regulations and rates change so frequently that a manual such as this cannot hope to provide the most up-to-date information. Yet a publications director must become familiar with many of these regulations or risk having publications rejected as outsized or paying higher than necessary mailing costs. A drawn-out dispute with the Postal Service over the inclusion of college catalogs as second-class matter has been settled, and most institutions should establish a second-class series for their catalogs and admissions materials. Obtain a copy of the *Postal Service Manual* and supplements, and talk over postal problems with your local postmaster.

24. Continually reexamine your program. A publication that does no harm but very little good is too costly to continue. A sunset law for college and university publications might be a good idea; each year we should be asked to justify the purpose and evaluate the effectiveness of each publication before we go ahead with a new edition. We should look for publications that have outlived their usefulness, that can be combined with other publications, or that can be produced every two or three years instead of every year.

25. Spend enough to do the job right. Every printed piece that you publish is designed to produce a positive impact that results in action. You recruit students, you raise money, you sell concert tickets, you influence foundations. Any publication, no matter how cheap, that fails to do an effective communications job is a total waste of money.

Many college publications directors can honestly say that they save their institutions more each year than they receive in salary. But they do not achieve these results and maintain high editorial standards without a serious and continuing study of the printing field.

Chapter 17

The New Technology

Kelvin J. Arden

He who first shortened the labour of Copyists by device of *Movable Types* was disbanding hired Armies, and cashiering most Kings and Senates, and creating a whole new Democratic world: He had invented the Art of Printing (Thomas Carlyle, *Sartor Resartus,* 1833).

Peering into the future is an entertaining and usually harmless pursuit—unless, of course, you invest in the wrong stocks, install the wrong equipment, or prepare yourself for a vanishing profession. When we are dealing with the technology of communication, surprises have run well ahead of popular predictions.

This chapter was first written 13 years ago and, to be on the safe side (the writer thought), even had a tongue-in-cheek look at what might happen to college publications in 1999. Little did we anticipate fax machines in nearly every business office, even in motels and airports. Nor did we anticipate that many institutions would be sending professionally produced full-color videotapes to prospective students. Faster? Yes. Slicker? Yes. More effective? Well, let's wait and see.

Some elements of our profession change slowly, if at all. What we put in type reads about the same as it has for many years. Development copy is still overblown and flaccid, course descriptions are often misleading, and student recruitment materials sometimes sound more like Disney World than an academic institution.

But overall we have come a long way and, with the 21st century looming closer every day, some of our best guesses may turn out to be right. One thing is for sure: The new technology will be full of surprises.

There is some question today as to whether the new technology of graphic communications will work *for* us or work *on* us. There are many indications that, unless we run very fast, we wind up as slave rather than master. Many of us have already heard the whip of an ever-demanding computer complex crack across our campuses. It would be pleasant if we could just stand back and wonder at these scientific marvels and then go back to the comfortable days of the old print shop. Perhaps unfortunately, if we are in the communications business, we are going to have to make our peace with what has been called the "gee whiz hardware."

Computers and cathode ray tubes are replacing the old gang in the composing room, and electronic scanners are taking the place of the critical eye of the master pressman. Of course these changes aren't all going to happen overnight, or even next year, and not entirely even 10 or 20 years from now. Progress in the graphic communications field has come through evolution, not revolution. And every technical change has come about for economic reasons. The publishers of medium-sized newspapers do not install $100,000 phototypesetting systems unless they are sure they will pay off.

The craftsmanship involved in communications graphics and college publications is rapidly moving from the printer into the hands of the designer and editor. With the automation of many printing processes, the craftsmanship that goes into a magazine, for example, must be supplied by the artists, photographers, and designers in the publishing office. All the elements of graphic quality go in before a single press rolls.

In a sense we have been moving away from individual craftsmanship ever since Gutenberg printed his first book with movable type. Every development in the printing industry since then has been to remove the hand of man and substitute the machine. The artisan has been transformed by the economic force of mass communication into a supervisor of electronic equipment.

Before we shed too many tears for the fading vision of the old-time printer gamely battling automation with the trusty platen press, we might have a look at the future. It must first be granted that today the printing industry is at an awkward transitional stage, caught between a 400-year-old tradition and the new age of electronic communication. But once we are over the hurdle of justifying the new techniques for economic reasons alone, the creative possibilities for producing exciting graphic materials are enormous.

Electronic layout systems are now found in most university printing plants and have replaced the ubiquitous typewriter in publications offices. A position title has already been created for the staff members who operate this equipment as the following excerpt from the typographical publication *U&lc* predicted years ago.

> The Typographics Director, operating the keyboard, will call up onto a TV-like screen all the elements that comprise the page, ad, or area being worked on.
>
> Each will be positioned, via keyboard instruction. The more capable machines will display text and headlines in their correct size and style and will size pictorial elements and position them too. The screen will display the layout, giving the designer a preview of how the job will look. Less sophisticated machines will *simulate* type styles, leave space for illustrations and pictures, and may represent the area to scale in less than actual size.
>
> In many cases, when the typographic director previews the basic lay-

out he/she will be able to electronically change the selection, size and position of the elements. Paper proofs can be produced of the final version or of any variation wanted for future reference. When the layout is finally approved, it can be stored for future use or further revisions, printed out immediately on paper or film, or sent as information to the typesetting unit where it will cause the type to be set and positioned as per the layout.

These electronic layout systems will increase the designers' productivity, make it easier to create and view alternative solutions, and expedite their final production. But, as fantastic as the machines are they won't exercise design judgment. They are only slaves and to maximize their value they will need a creative person with an understanding and appreciation of typography to command them—a typographics director. . . . Graphic arts quality is entering the office of the future. Here will be found the typographics director, the information manager, the director of communications—and others.

Among the "others" we must assume will be college publications directors and university editors.

The college catalog of the future

It might be a therapeutic mental exercise for those of us who sometimes feel we are losing our never-ending battle for printing quality to take a look at some publications in the future. These future images were first projected 20 years ago, and this writer suspects that they will still be on the publications horizon in 2001.

Let's take a look at what may happen to some of our publications in 2001. There's nothing special about that year except that it's far enough away to make speculation safe. Our most costly publication and one that has defied almost all real change for more than a hundred years is the catalog.

In 2001 we might see a campus scene something like this: John Jones, a freshman, has just arrived and is entering the student services building, which in 1979 was the university bookstore and in 1909 was the school chapel. Inside the lobby he stops at a row of telephones over which is a sign saying, "Information for Incoming Students." His questions are answered by a pleasant but slightly mechanical-sounding voice, and this voice directs him to the "Program Coordinating Center."

Here he presents a small plastic card containing his identification credentials, his scholarship or loan fund rating, and his complete secondary school record. After waiting a bit, he is met by an attractive young admissions technician and led into a cubicle furnished with two chairs and a small computer input unit.

The freshman and the technician chat a moment before the technician produces a small envelope containing several punched cards. These cards represent the results of a battery of aptitude and interest tests John has taken plus predetermined coding for the study programs he thinks he may wish to enter. The admissions technician glances over the punched cards and then feeds them one at a time into the computer input unit. John is then told to wait in the outer office until his name is called.

While John bites his fingernails and the admissions technician is sipping a cup of coffee, the latest in a long line of computer generations is humming away, turning out a personalized college catalog. In a matter of seconds, John's record is analyzed, his ambitions weighed, and a variety of options decided upon. The computer center itself is a few miles off campus in a specially designed facility, but through a system of input and printout stations it reaches into every department of the university.

The printout unit in the admissions office is an advanced model that can electronically generate up to 20,000 graphic characters per second. An office worker gathers up the 50 or so pages of John's catalog, puts them into a plastic binder, and calls his name. As our new student picks up his 2001 catalog, he notices that his photograph, name, and identification number are printed on the first page. The following pages include pictures and background sketches of his faculty and student adviser, as well as a campus map, which indicates all the buildings in which he will study and his living unit.

Course descriptions in his program areas are several pages long and contain information on the teaching approach of each professor as well as library research codes.

Pipe dreams? Perhaps, but still possible with the communications technology that already is at hand.

Just as TV did not supplant radio or the motion pictures, we are certain that its more sophisticated uses will not drive out newspapers, magazines, or even college catalogs. The range of means to communicate will be much wider, but each new technology advance will fill a particular niche depending upon effectiveness, cost, and public appeal.

The electronic annual report

For purposes of probing the foggy future, let us picture a scene in 2001 in which a university has decided to forgo the traditional printed annual report in favor of an electronic message.

The annual report has just arrived in the mail. It has been sent in a small box just three by four inches wide and about half an inch thick. This size caused some consternation in the development office as they figured that some wealthy old-timers might miss it in a stack of junk mail. Sad to say, the 2001 Postal Service has yet to solve many long-standing problems.

After sorting through her monthly bills, alumna Susan Smith opens the little box from her alma mater and finds a videotape cartridge. One side of the plastic container is marked Picture Side 1; the other, Video Printout Side 2. After dinner the alumna calls her family into the den and switches on the VCR. A large screen hidden in the wall flashes on. She inserts the annual report tape, and the sound of the alma mater fills the room, along with color views of the campus.

The nostalgic introduction fades away and is quickly followed by a closeup of the president. "Alumni and friends of the university," the president begins, "it is indeed a rare personal privilege to be able to visit with you in your homes and to bring to you in word and picture the events and achievements of a challenging year." Helping the president tell the story for the videotape audience are a number of his key administrators, some outstanding faculty, and a panel of carefully selected students.

As the highlights of the year unfold, pictures of the actual happenings are cut into the taped report. The alumna and her family see some action shots from the homecoming football game, the dedication of a new space sanitation laboratory, and some on-location pictures of an underseas experimental farm. A year of university activities is compressed into a half-hour show.

Any portion of the taped report may be seen as often as the viewer wishes and may also be shown to friends or groups of prospective students.

At the conclusion of Side 1, the president invites the audience to use the second side in their video printout system for a graphic reproduction of the university's financial report. The video printout unit electronically generates images for balance sheets, charts, and graphs. These images are reproduced on paper by electrostatic printing, and in a matter of minutes the alumna has a sheaf of multicolor documents to ponder. All of the graphics in the financial report are produced by a computer programmed to design and develop graphic interpretations from statistical analysis.

The more things change. . .

There are those of us who will miss the smell of fresh ink and the thump and clatter of a good sturdy press. We can hope that even in the 21st century some independent souls will happily be feeding paper into a well-polished Chandler and Price. But for those who must survive in the changing world of publications, knowledge of computers, electronic media, and the new technology will be essential.

Techniques have now been perfected and systems developed that can completely change the way we communicate. How fast these changes will be adopted depends upon how much they are needed or how competitively advantageous they will be. One thing is certain: It is no longer a question of *whether* we are to become involved in the new technology, but *when*.

The videotaped annual report of 2001, if wisely produced, could be an institution's most important communication effort. But the new technology will not answer the old editorial questions of what to put in and what to leave out. While the futurists depict a communications table overflowing with an assortment of electronic goodies, the task of the publications person will remain constant—choosing words and pictures, whether they are to be displayed by ink on paper or by a beam of electrons focused on the face of a cathode ray tube. The task is to communicate as effectively as possible to a variety of audiences.

Chapter 18

From Composing Sticks to Computers: An Afterword

William J. Whalen

After 40 years as a publications director, I think I'm finally starting to get the hang of it. But I've made my share of mistakes, and I wish I had known a few more things when I started my career.

Here are a handful of observations, anecdotes, and guidelines I'd like to offer for your consideration.

Play fair. Play fair with typesetters and printers. Years ago I heard a publications director from a university in Michigan describe his formula for getting low-cost printing. He always got 10 bids on every job because he was sure that at least one estimator out of 10 would make a mistake. He may have saved a few dollars here and there, but in the long run, taking advantage of a vendor's honest mistake is no way to build a list of reliable, quality-oriented vendors.

Likewise, expect fair play in return. Say goodbye to vendors who switch paper stock, concoct alteration charges, or tell too many fibs.

Disputes are inevitable. Realize that disputes between printer and client are inevitable. Some professors and deans who seldom buy printing expect perfection. If the halftone on page 19 lacks the snap they expect or the second color isn't exactly the shade they wanted, they may demand that the printer redo the entire booklet.

Obviously, the typical printer, operating on a modest profit margin and getting work on a competitive bid system, cannot afford to redo many jobs and stay in business. I suggest a cooling-off period after delivery of a job. By that time, the client may have mellowed and realized that the job is not that bad after all or at least not so bad that a reasonable price adjustment will not suffice.

On occasions when the printer really goofs—prints green ink where red was specified, uses matte finish instead of enamel, mixes up page numbers or photo captions—you have no choice but to insist on a reprint.

In a sense, you must protect the client from the printer and the printer from the client. The publications specialist can encourage honest negotiation and arrive at a solution to reprint or accept a price break and live with less than perfection.

Do your homework. Do your homework before your choose a printer. By matching jobs to printers, you can probably save your institution a lot of money. Local printers may be fine, but don't overlook the cost advantages of printers far away from your campus. Using overnight mail, the fax machine, and the telephone, you can complete these jobs with few headaches. We have had a quicker turnaround on a 400-page graduate catalog printed in Texas than we have had from a larger printer 25 miles from my office.

Avoid off-the-cuff estimates. People are always calling me to ask how much their booklets will cost. Often they haven't decided on format, colors, number of halftones, or even quantity. I sometimes counter by asking them what a three-bedroom house costs. It all depends.

Unless we have just done an identical job, I ask the client for a couple of days to get an estimate. From bitter experience, I know that if I give an off-the-cuff answer, I may be quoted in a committee as saying a job will cost $2,000. Then, when the final cost exceeds $3,000, everyone gets cranky. A publication is a tailor-made product with many variables. Asking for a little extra time to get an estimate is reasonable—and a good way to avoid messy situations.

Avoid change for change's sake. I have heard of admissions directors who insist on completely new photos in every edition of their prospectus even though the books go to a different group of high school students each year. These directors are bound to replace some first-rate photos with some that are less attractive.

Of course, if your alumni tabloid looks just like it did 20 years ago, you've failed to keep up with design styles. But if you change completely every three or four years, you may risk losing your identity. Take a tip from the commercial world. How often has *Time* magazine changed its cover format? Or *Reader's Digest?* Or *National Geographic?*

Take the initiative. Don't wait for projects to come to you. Some publications officers sit back and take it easy until clients come through the door with projects. I have always believed that one of the chief responsibilities of a publications department is to study its institution's needs and see which ones it can meet with printed materials.

When the publications department discovers the needs, the director must do the politicking to get the funds. On the other hand, when a publication no longer serves its purpose, the director must be heartless in killing it.

Share ideas with colleagues. Get together with other people in your field to share ideas. For almost three decades, the publications directors from the Big Ten schools and the University of Chicago have been meeting once a year for this reason. The University of Notre Dame, Washington University, Iowa State University, and Pennsylvania State University have also joined our group. This type of sharing and networking is invaluable. Every fall we set an agenda, meet on one of our campuses, share ideas and publications, compare budgets, discuss common problems, and exchange salary information.

If you don't participate in a similar consortium, why not organize one? Pick institutions in an athletic conference or a particular state or region, but limit membership to the dozen or so directors who can sit comfortably around a table.

Just say no (sometimes). Don't be afraid to discourage publication at times. You can't meet every need with a publication. The head of a specialized department once wanted to send a two-color poster and post cards to a thousand colleges and universities to advertise for two graduate instructors. We persuaded him to send 40 letters to his counterparts at other universities instead. He quickly got two excellent candidates.

Go slowly with newsletters. View newsletters with suspicion. I have seen so many newsletters come and go over the years that I always ask the client to rethink the need. Typically, someone or some committee gets the idea for a newsletter. Filling Volume 1, No. 1 is no problem. But enthusiasm wanes as Nos. 2 and 3 come along, and by the time you reach No. 6 or 7, putting out a regular newsletter has become just another chore. The easy access to desktop publishing has only exacerbated the problem. Often a booklet or leaflet will give all the information the client thought would fill a series of newsletters.

Watch your writing. Pay just as much attention to writing as you do to design. Several decades ago, almost anything other than black ink or gray stock stood out in college and university publications. But today, after revolutionary advancements in graphic design, the winners from CASE and UCDA (University and College Designers Association) competitions could hold their own in any design contest. Photo quality is also noticeably higher.

What has not changed much is writing quality. It's not hard to figure out why. Typically you must take copy someone else has written and try to edit it into an acceptable form. Often you're trying to polish copy submitted by someone whose writing style has been permanently mangled by writing a doctoral dissertation.

Perhaps your publications office has been able to add designers to your staff and get professional photography and illustration, but few have the luxury of employing full-time writers.

To my mind, the next step in improving our publications should be to publish words that are as well-crafted as our design and photography. This costs money, and it may mean hiring a professional writer who'll need three or four weeks to research and write copy for a 32-page booklet. But the result will be worth it.

Confer with others. Arrange seminars for clients and high school students and counselors. If I had it to do over again, I would plan more seminars. The ones we've sponsored have been worthwhile, but they've often received low priority in the race to get publications delivered.

When we hold a seminar for clients, we invite a dozen regular customers to discuss how we can help them and how they can help us. About two hours over coffee and doughnuts gives us time to explore several areas. Likewise, lunch with a half-dozen high school students or high school counselors could tell you more about the effectiveness of your student recruitment publications than a mail survey.

Appreciate the appreciative client. Bless the client who says, "I need your help. You're the professional." Fortunately, most of our clients fall into this category.

But a few take a different attitude: "The committee has worked out the design, and we would like you to get it printed," they may say. Or "My wife took art in college and has done the cover illustration." Or "The dean said you could not change one word of this copy."

In situations such as these, you may choose to work closely with the 95 percent who want your professional help and just go along with the 5 percent who think they can do a better job than your editors and designers. Occasionally you will have to go to the mat, but you cannot afford to spend much of your time battling for lost causes. Some people will always prefer *Bowling for Dollars* to *Masterpiece Theatre,* and you are not likely to change their taste.

Learn and teach. Take advantage of the courses your institution offers. A publications specialist today needs many different skills. Most institutions, no matter how small, offer courses in management, accounting, marketing, writing, organizational communication, graphic design, computer science, and journalism. One of my colleagues earned two master's degrees, one in English and one in communication, while working full time in the publications office.

Teach an occasional class even though it takes a lot of time. I think teaching is time well spent if you use the classroom experience to sharpen your own editing, writing, or design skills. It will also help you keep in touch with the fundamental reason why your institution exists: to educate young men and women.

I have taught writing classes to about 1,700 students since 1950, and I have quizzed almost every one on why he or she chose to enroll at Purdue. It helps me get some insight into why someone makes this important decision.

Keep up. Make a daily effort to keep abreast of new technology. Nothing is more certain than change. Not much changed in typesetting and printing from the invention of the Linotype until the 1950s, but now the new technology can make your knowledge obsolete in a few years.

I'd suggest attending CASE conferences and workshops; visiting typesetters, printers, paper companies; reading several of the better periodicals in design and desktop publishing; and taking advantage of any courses in computers offered by your institution or other organizations in your community.

Don't job-hop (unless you must). Don't make the mistake of thinking that the only way you can challenge yourself is by changing jobs. People call me various names, but one they have never used is "job-hopper." The decision to move is easy if you find yourself in a dead-end job or in constant conflict with your boss.

But it isn't necessary to change jobs to add excitement and new challenges to your life. Since I started at Purdue in 1950, I have seen the enrollment at our West Lafayette campus triple and the publications staff grow from three to 26 people. I have worked for nine bosses—a new one approximately every four and a half years. These changes have given me all the challenge I wanted.

Don't expect to get rich. If you've entered advancement work for the money, I suggest you head for the development area. Every salary survey shows that development people make more than those of us who work in publications, alumni relations, or news bureaus.

To me, though, the satisfaction of seeing a publication go from concept to delivered piece outweighs the monetary edge of development jobs.

Working for a college or university not only has the obvious advantages—indoor work with no heavy lifting—but also the satisfaction of participating in the exciting enterprise of educating the young and advancing knowledge. Personally, I don't think I would have gotten the same kicks anywhere else.

An earlier version of this chapter appeared in the February 1986 CURRENTS.

How to Break into Print

A *number of colleges and universities publish publications guides for their faculty and staff. With a few modifications this Appendix reproduces* Your Guide to Better Publications, *prepared by the Office of Publications of Purdue University.*

People judge Purdue University mainly by the quality of its teaching, research, and service, but many other factors influence impressions. Among these are architecture, landscaping, athletic programs, cultural opportunities, public relations, and the University's publications.

We expect a first-class institution such as Purdue to publish first-class materials. We allow no concession for amateur graphics, poor legibility, dull copy, inaccuracies, out-of-date information, or washed-out photos. The Office of Publications (OOP) strives for quality.

The University established this department in 1925 as the University Editor's Office and later renamed it the Office of Publications. In its time this office has seen many changes. For example, some requirements, such as affirmative action and disclaimer statements, were unknown even 20 years ago, but they form an important part of the office's responsibilities today.

In a typical year OOP will produce more than 400 publications—brochures, books, posters, leaflets, and others. At any given time our office has from 60 to 115 publications in production. Some of these are all-University publications, such as catalogs or the campus map which are funded in the publications budget, but the OOP edits and designs many others for various University schools, departments, and offices. The OOP makes no charges for editorial or design services.

With several exceptions the office also is responsible for checking copy on all publications printed by Printing Services or commercial vendors. The University has instructed these printers not to proceed with such jobs without a signed OK from the OOP. This instruction does not extend to office forms, student publications, tickets, newsletters, and similar types of printed matter.

Before you come here

Submit your text, typed and double-spaced, on 8½ - x 11-inch paper with one-inch margins on each side and the bottom.

Begin the first page of the text one-third of the page from the top.

Prepare completed copy as neatly as possible. Avoid making extensive corrections in the margins after the text has been typed.

Do not attach any copy to the manuscript with cellophane tape or staples. We suggest that you use transparent tape or rubber cement.

Clients may be asked to provide more acceptable copy if the original copy is typed single-spaced or handwritten, if extensive corrections have been penned in, or if copy is not legible.

Mark copy in pencil rather than ink.

Whenever you feel that clearance of copy is necessary, obtain it from deans, department heads, committees, or colleagues *before* the manuscript goes to the typesetter.

Copy will not be accepted piecemeal. We will begin to schedule and produce your publication after we receive *all* copy, including photos, illustrations, and captions.

Keep it simple

Though an editor will review your manuscript, you can get your text off to a good start by examining it yourself for style, accuracy, spelling, grammar, punctuation, and syntax. You are on safe ground if you use simple, direct sentences and active, not passive, verbs. Write for your particular audience. Teenage prospective students, for example, will probably not respond to prose couched in professional or bureaucratic terms and phrases.

Short sentences improve readability. If the average length of your sentences exceeds 17 words, you will discourage potential readers who do not have college degrees. Complex grammatical constructions will also hurt readability.

In general, avoid unnecessary words, educational jargon, foreign phrases, and abstractions. Prefer the familiar to the unfamiliar word.

How to start

Make your first contact with the director of publications; if the director is unavailable, please contact the associate director. The director will assign an editor and designer to work with you. Editors and designers are instructed not to accept new jobs from clients who have not been so assigned. The editor is responsible for coordinating production of your publication among several persons—you, the designer, the typesetter, the printer, and others. When you have any questions, check with the editor.

At your first meeting with the editor and designer, you will help fill out a publication planning guide, determining such information as the intended readers of the publication, number of copies to be printed, delivery date, budget limitations, etc. Depending on the job, you may meet further with the assigned editor and designer to work out details.

How much will it cost?

The Office of Publications avoids giving "ball park" estimates because each publication is a tailor-made product. When specifications have been completed, we will be happy to get bids.

Most of the composition and printing jobs for the publications produced by the Office of Publications go to the low bidder. The office solicits bids from vendors throughout the state and tries to match their capabilities with the requirements of the job. Allow up to a week for preparation of specifications and a week to receive bids from vendors. Complicated jobs may require more time. Working from the planning guide, the editor and designer will prepare specifications for your job.

Unauthorized work with outside vendors

Individual faculty and staff members are not authorized to contract for writing, design, photography, or printing with outside vendors. If they make such arrangements without prior approval of the Purchasing Department, they may be asked to pay for such services with a personal check.

The six graphic designers in the Office of Publications can handle most publication design assignments. Only if these designers cannot meet a reasonable deadline will Purchasing authorize the employment of a free-lance designer or design firm.

The director of the OOP can recommend several free-lance designers whose work and prices meet University standards. Please check with the director after you get cost estimates and before you commit University funds to such work.

Required paperwork and authorizations

The editor with whom you are working will describe necessary paperwork to start your job. For publications going to commercial typesetters and printers we need a signed Form 12 Rev. (purchase requisition) for each vendor. This form should be sent or delivered directly to the Office of Publications before work can proceed; sending the form to the Purchasing Department only delays your job since it will be rerouted to the OOP anyway.

You should give the publication's title and the quantity on this form, but the editor will fill in detailed specifications. If the publication will be printed by the University's Printing Services, you must furnish a signed work order. The designer will be happy to help you prepare specifications for this work order.

How long will delivery take?

An average publication such as a 32-page booklet could take eight to ten weeks for delivery from the date you submit completed copy. If the publication requires extensive design, add one or two weeks to this schedule. This assumes that the client will provide immediate proofreading of galleys and pages and will not make major changes in text or design after type has been set or design finalized. Jobs going through the office during the Thanksgiving and Christmas holidays will take somewhat longer than average.

Each publication is tailor-made. Allow ample time for the many production steps in order to conserve the University's printing dollar and to minimize chances of error. After copy has been written and the planning guide has been prepared, a typical job will involve the following steps: editing by OOP editors, designing, bidding, obtaining Form 12s or work orders, typesetting, proofreading, returning galleys to the typesetter for reproduction proofs, proofreading any corrections on repro proofs, preparing keylines or completed paste-ups, client approval of paste-up, sending paste-up to the printer, checking the blueline or page proof, returning for revisions (if necessary), giving OK to print, printing, binding, and delivery.

Why editing is important

OOP editors carry many responsibilities with each publication. They assume responsibility for guiding each publication from that first planning session through delivery. They not only perform copy editing; they also review a publication for structure and organization.

Good editing organizes the written material for unity, coherence, and emphasis. OOP editors consult the Office of Publications style section of this manual and other generally accepted standards for punctuation, syntax, rules of grammar, and spelling. They also review copy for accuracy, timeliness, completeness, and good taste.

We've got style

When submitting copy for publications to be processed by the OOP, follow the University's style in the style section of this manual. This section, however, is not intended to serve as a complete style manual, because it only highlights some areas of particular concern to Purdue University. Otherwise, the Office of Publications generally follows *The Chicago Manual of Style.*

Why graphic design is important

The design staff of the Office of Publications takes pride in professionally designed publications which not only have won prizes in national competition but also have won praise from campus clients and their readers.

Good graphic design enhances communication. It can attract attention and pull readers into the publication's message. Graphic designers give abstract ideas visual form. They develop formats that organize information, and select papers, inks, and styles of illustration to complement your message. Graphic design plays a vital role in producing effective communication.

Design services

Graphic designers in the OOP will assist any University school, department, or office in its design needs. However, the OOP functions as a publications office rather than as an art-design service. We must limit our design services to those publications for which we assume editorial responsibility.

We do not have enough people to provide a general art and design service to produce signs, charts, advertisements, slides, illustrations, teaching aids, etc., but our designers will be happy to suggest sources on and off campus for such work.

Photographs

The assistant director for photography and the photojournalist provide photos for publications of the Office of Publications and its sister departments in University Relations. In most cases the photographers will take photos for other departments. Otherwise, clients should contact photographic services in the Center for Instructional Services.

If you are using prints from your own files, remember that Polaroid photos and color slides converted into black and white halftones seldom meet quality standards.

Due to the high cost of color film and processing, it will be necessary for the Office of Publications to receive a cost-only reimbursement for these items.

Proofreading

The client bears the main responsibility for proofreading galleys and pages. Each proof should be initialed to avoid any misunderstandings. Please use the standard proofreading symbols found in this manual and in most dictionaries.

Author's alterations

Typesetters do not charge for correcting their own errors, but they must charge for changes made at the customer's request. The cost of revising galley and page proofs has gone up greatly in recent years. Changing a single comma or word can easily cost $10 or more because of the time charges for resetting, proofreading, etc. You will help conserve the University's printing dollar by keeping author's alterations to a minimum. The best advice is: edit typewritten text, not galley proofs.

Putting it all together

Preparation of keylines or completed paste-ups for offset printing should be considered part of the manufacturing process. Most typesetters who do Purdue work can take a rough dummy and turn it into camera-ready art. Our graphic designers keep busy creating designs and preparing keylines for all-University publications. Occasionally, they can spare the time to do the keylining of a client's publication, but they do not automatically assume this responsibility. When they have a backlog of creative design work, they will ask the vendors to include the cost of paste-up in the bids.

Page proofs and the OK to print

We will ask you to review and to approve the completed paste-up, chiefly to make sure that all of the elements—type, photos, headlines, and art—are in their proper places. The printer will provide a page proof, which again we will ask you to review and to sign or initial, chiefly to make sure that the printer has made no errors.

Overs and unders

Printers try to print exactly the number of copies that you ordered, but to make certain that they have enough good or acceptable copies, they sometimes will run more copies than the order. Sometimes they may end up with fewer good copies than were ordered. Long-standing trade practices limit these "overs and unders" to 10 percent of the order. Sometimes a client must have no fewer than a certain number and this must be stipulated on the bid and purchase order so that the printer will not deliver the job with a 10 percent underrun.

Distribution of publications

The Office of Publications mailing room handles U.S. and campus mailings of publications for which the office is responsible. The mailing room must meet the requirements for second-, third-, and fourth-class mail and must prepare mail shipments according to U.S. post office regulations. The publications office does not operate a general mailing service for materials it does not edit and design; please make such arrangements with Printing Services.

Sample copies

Vendors are instructed to send six copies of each publication directly to the Office of Publications for the president, the vice president for university relations, office archives, and editor/designer files.

Official University seal

The Office of Publications is responsible for monitoring use of the official University seal on University publications. The office will provide reproduction proofs of the seal in various sizes as well as a sheet of instructions. The seal should not be used with additional borders, ornamentation, or overprinting, nor should other logos incorporate elements of the seal. If the seal or some other University logo is to be used on merchandise, the manufacturer must enter into a licensing arrangement with the Purdue Research Foundation.

Stationery and business cards

All schools, departments, offices, and other agencies of the University will use letterheads and envelopes printed according to standards established for official University stationery. The vice president for university relations has overall responsibility for the consistent application of these standards and will act on all requests for exceptions.

Printing Services has established the type-style and format for official business cards. Exceptions to these standards must be approved by the director of publications.

Publications of the Office of Publications

The Office of Publications works with all schools and departments on campus, but it also has many publications of an all-University nature for which it is responsible. Some of these are the catalogs, *Introduction to Purdue, Purdue Reports, Sercle, Welcome to Purdue* campus map, *Financial Report, Religious Life at Purdue,* schedules of classes, summer sessions booklet, admissions booklets, *Faculty and Staff Handbook, Faculty and Staff Roster, General Information,* Purdue University Press books, a series of financial aid publications, *Perspective, Purdue Today, Guide to*

News and Publications Services, University Regulations, and this booklet, *Your Guide to Better Publications.*

Perspective

The Office of Publications publishes the 16-page tabloid, *Perspective.* This quarterly newspaper goes to more than 240,000 alumni, parents of students, and staff members. The associate director of publications serves as editor.

Purdue Today

Purdue Today, a biweekly tabloid, contains news and feature items of interest and importance to Purdue faculty and administrative/professional staffs at the West Lafayette and regional campuses. Faculty and staff members are encouraged to send news items and suggestions for feature stories to the editor.

Sercle

Sercle is a monthly tabloid of four pages with *Purdue Preview* calendar included 10 months of the year. It contains news and items of interest to the service and clerical staffs of the West Lafayette and regional campuses. News items and suggestions can be sent to the editor.

Other publications offices

Other campus offices besides the Office of Publications produce publications. The publications section of the Agricultural Communication Service publishes hundreds of bulletins each year for the Agricultural Experiment Station and the Cooperative Extension Service. The Engineering Productions Office handles some publications for the Schools of Engineering. The Purdue Alumni Association publishes the *Purdue Alumnus* nine times a year. An independent nonprofit corporation, the Purdue Student Publishing Foundation, publishes the *Purdue Exponent* daily during the regular school year and three times a week during summer sessions.

["How to Keep in Style," reproduced on the following pages, is Purdue's style guide. It differs only slightly from CASE's style, which is followed in this book.]

How to keep in style

I. Capitalization

When in doubt, do not capitalize.

Capitalize

1.1   Proper nouns, months. days of the week, but not the seasons.

1.2   All words, except articles, conjunctions, and prepositions in the titles of books, plays, lectures, musical compositions, etc., including *A* and *The* if at the beginning of the title.

   The Man Who Came to Dinner

   "On the Response of the Timoshenko Beam to a Gaussian Stochastic Process"

1.3   All conferred and traditional educational, occupational, and business titles when used specifically in front of the name or in lists and programs; do not capitalize these titles in the text when they follow the name, unless the title is a named or distinguished professorship. (See also, Section V. Titles)

   Frederick R. Ford, executive vice president and treasurer, or Vice President Frederick R. Ford

   Prof. Alice Jones is head of the Department of Fabric Technology

   L. M. Warshawsky, chief of the Analog Computation Branch, Wright-Patterson Air Force Base, or Chief L. M. Warshawsky of the Analog Computation Branch, Wright-Patterson Air Force Base

   Samuel Brown, Moss Professor of Engineering and professor of civil engineering

1.4   The word *University*, whenever referring to Purdue University, even though the word *Purdue* may not precede it.

1.5   The words *Army, Navy*, and *Air Force*, when referring to United States armed forces, whether or not preceded by the letters *U.S.*

1.6   The words *association, building, center, club, conference, department, division, hall, office, senate, street, university*, etc., when used as part of a title; thereafter, do not capitalize the words *association, building*, etc., when used alone to refer to that specific place or group.

   the University Senate—thereafter, the senate

   the Department of Physics—thereafter, the department

   the East Faculty Lounge—thereafter, the lounge

   the Achievement Center—thereafter, the center

   the West Lafayette Campus—thereafter, the campus

1.7   Board of Trustees—thereafter, the board or the trustees.

1.8   A specific course or subject. such as: ENGL 525. Middle English.

1.9   Entire geographical names.

   the Wabash River

   Turkey Run State Park

1.10   Geographical regions of the country. but not points of the compass.

   the South, the Midwest, the East

   northeast

1.11   Names of athletic clubs and teams.

   the Boilermakers

   the Chicago Cubs

1.12   Names of all races and nationalities (see also 1.16).

   Caucasian, Nigerian, Irish, Japanese

1.13   The word *room* when used to designate a particular room.

   Room 309 of the Heine Pharmacy Building

1.14   Official college degrees when spelled out (see also 1.22).

   Bachelor of Science in Agriculture

   Doctor of Philosophy

1.15   Named, distinguished, and similar professorships.

Do not capitalize

1.16 Designations based on color. size. or local usage.

black	white	pygmy	redneck

1.17 Titles standing alone or in apposition.

The dean of the School of Management must approve all research projects.

Contact the dean of students for further information.

Alice Jones. professor of English. will speak at the symposium.

1.18 Names of school or college studies, fields of study, options. curricula. major areas. major subjects. or programs. except names of languages. unless a specific course is being referred to (see also 1.8).

He is studying philosophy and English.

Each student must meet core requirements in science and the humanities.

Purdue offers a curriculum in industrial education.

The School of Agriculture offers degrees in the following fields of specialization: animal sciences. horticulture. etc.

1.19 Organized groups or classes of students in a university or high school, or the words *freshman, sophomore. junior,*

senior. or graduate. when they refer to the year in which a course is to be taken or to the classification of the student.

ENGL 101 should be taken in the freshman year.

John Smith is a junior in the School of Science.

The senior class will conduct its annual election tomorrow.

1.20 Unofficial titles preceding the name.

guitarist Julian Bream

1.21 Designations of officers of a class, social organization. etc.

Paula Smith is president of the Purdue Women's Dinner Club.

She was elected freshman class secretary.

1.22 These words or abbreviations:

a.m.	honors
p.m.	line
baccalaureate	master's degree
doctor's degree	page
federal	paragraph
government	state

1.23 The words *offices. schools.* and *departments* when referring to more than one individual office, school, or department.

schools of Veterinary Medicine and Chemical Engineering (but Schools of Engineering)

II. Abbreviations

When in doubt, spell word out.

Abbreviate

2.1 The following titles when they precede a name: Dr., Mr., Mrs., the Rev., Fr., and all military titles.

2.2 Other titles, such as professor, only when they precede the first name or initials; spell out titles when they are used before the surname alone.

Prof. E. B. Smith

Professor Smith

Profs. E. B. Smith and J. T. Jones

Professors Smith and Jones

2.3 Page to p. or pp. in footnotes or bibliographical material: spell out when used in text material (page not Page).

2.4 Eastern standard time as EST. without periods.

2.5 *And* as an ampersand (&) only in corporate titles.

2.6 The word *Saint* when used to refer to such cities as St. Louis. St. Paul etc.

2.7 Complimentary titles. such as Mr., Mrs., and Dr.. but do not use them in combination with any other title or with abbreviations indicating scholastic or academic degrees.

Paul Huston. Ph.D., not Dr. Paul Huston. Ph.D.

Carol Green. M.D., or Roger White. D.V.M., not Dr. Carol Green. M.D., or Mr. Roger White. D.V.M.

2.8 The degrees *Bachelor of Science. Master of Science. Master of Arts. Doctor of Philosophy.* and *Educational Specialist.* to B.S., M.S., M.A., Ph.D.. and Ed.S.. with periods.

2.9 The department name of a course when it is followed by the course number.

Besides an elective course in English. MA 333 should be selected by the student.

2.10 When it is necessary to use a subject-matter designation and course number to identify a specific course, e.g., MA 111. use the official subject-matter abbreviation. If you are in doubt about what these designations are. contact the Office of Schedules and Space.

Do not abbreviate

2.11   Names of countries, other than U.S.A. and U.S.S.R.

2.12   Given names, such as George. William, and Charles.

2.13   Names of states, when following names of cities and towns, except in footnotes.

     West Lafayette, Indiana

     Use post office designations for states only in addresses on mailings.

2.14   The words *association, avenue, boulevard, department, institute, street,* etc.

2.15   Names of months.

2.16   Christmas in the form of Xmas.

2.17   The word percent.

In general use the word percent, but in scientific, technical, and statistical copy use the symbol %

     Of this year's student enrollment, 60 percent are men and 40 percent are women.

     Reports of spirocercosis in dogs vary from 2% to 100% of the canine population examined.

     Boston showed an 8.1% drop and Pittsburgh a 13.9% drop in population from 1970 to 1980. Jacksonville, Florida, grew by 150.8%, the largest percentage increase among the nation's larger cities.

2.18   Parts of geographic names, except Saint in St. Louis, St. Paul, etc., unless they are used in tabular matter

     Fort Wayne

     North Dakota

2.19   Assistant and associate when used in a title, such as assistant professor of bacteriology.

Note: abbreviations may be used more freely in tabular matter.

III. Punctuation

3.1   Use a comma before the words *and* and *or* in a series.

     The annual Gala Week show will be presented by the Varsity Glee Club, the Purduettes, and the Symphony Band.

3.2   Place a comma after digits signifying thousands: 1,150 students; except when reference is made to temperature: 4600 degrees.

3.3   Follow a statement that introduces a direct quotation of one or more paragraphs with a colon. Also use a colon after *as follows.*

3.4   Introductory words such as, *namely, i.e., e.g.,* and *viz* should be immediately preceded by a comma or semicolon and followed by a comma.

3.5   When listing names with cities or states, punctuate as follows: George Andrews, Frankfort, president; Carol Green, Lafayette, vice president; etc.

3.6   When abbreviating, punctuate with an apostrophe years of college classes.

     Class of '76

     John White, '39

3.7   Call letters of radio stations and alphabetical abbreviations of groups, organizations, or institutions such as WBAA, ROTC, USDA, MIT, or UCLA, should be capitalized and written without periods or space; but letter symbols of degrees, B.S., M.S., Ph.D. and of the U.S. or U.S.S.R. should be capitalized and written with periods.

3.8   Master's and doctor's degrees should always be written with an 's. Never write masters' degrees.

3.9   Hyphenate and place in quotation marks "All-American" when referring to Purdue's "All-American" Band.

3.10   Do not hyphenate the word *vice president* and words beginning with *non,* except those containing a proper noun.

     non-German

     nontechnical

3.11   Do not place a hyphen between the prefixes *pre. semi, anti,* etc., and nouns or adjectives, except proper nouns, but avoid duplicated vowels or triple consonants.

     predentistry   reapply   bell-like

     pro-American   pre-enroll

3.12   Do not place a hyphen between the prefix *sub* and the word to which it is attached.

     subtotal

3.13   Use a hyphen to avoid ambiguity.

     small-business profits, rather than small business profits.

3.14   Hyphenate *part-time* and *full-time* when used as adjectives, and hyphenate any modifying word combined with *well,* when preceding a noun.

     well-built engine

     well-grounded in mathematics

3.15   Hyphenate the word *X-ray* and use a capital X.

3.16   Use the nonhyphenated spelling of a word if either spelling is acceptable.

3.17 When writing a date, place a comma between the day, if given, and the year, and after the year. (see also 2.15)

December 25, 1987.

3.18 Do not place a comma between the month and year when the day is not mentioned. (see also 2.15)

December 1987

3.19 Italicize the titles of books, essays, long musical compositions, motion pictures, pamphlets, periodicals, etc., but place in quotation marks the titles of book series, radio and television programs (when part of a series), songs, lectures, and parts (chapters, titles of papers, etc.) of volumes.

3.20 Use single quotation marks for quotations printed within other quotations.

3.21 Use single quotation marks in headlines.

3.22 If several paragraphs are to be quoted, use quotation marks at the beginning of each paragraph but only at the end of the last paragraph.

3.23 Set quotation marks outside periods and commas and inside colons and semicolons. They should be set inside of exclamation points and interrogation marks that are not part of the quotation.

3.24 No quotation marks are necessary in printing interviews when the name of the speaker is given first, or in reports of testimony when the words *question* and *answer* or *Q* and *A* are used, such as:

Q: Who will benefit from the plan?
A: Full-time staff, students . . .

Jones: How do you plan your curriculum?
Smith: A committee does that.

IV. Figures

Use figures for

4.1 Numbers 10 or over, including ordinal numbers: 22nd.

4.2 Days of the month, omitting *rd, th, st, nd*: April 6, June 1.

4.3 Degrees

longitude 67° 03′ 06′′ W.

21.5° F below zero. (Omit the degree sign only in engineering and technical publications.)

4.4 Numbers within a series in order to maintain consistency if more than half of the numbers are 10 or over; otherwise spell out numbers within a series.

23 hours, 12 minutes, 6 seconds.

Twelve hats, five purses, five umbrellas, seven sweaters, and sixteen pairs of shoes were sold yesterday.

4.5 Sums that are cumbersome to spell out, but spell out the words *million* and *billion*.

5 3/4 million   17.9 billion

4.6 Write phone numbers as follows:

49-48745 for on-campus publications

494-8745 for publications going off campus

Avoiding unnecessary ciphers, use figures for

4.7 Hours of the day: 7 p.m. or 7:30 p.m. (never 7:00 p.m. unless used in lists of events, etc., to preserve alignment of type).

4.8 Amounts of money with the word cents or with the dollar sign: $3 (not $3.00), $5.09, or 77 cents, unless tabulated in columns.

4.9 Do not begin a sentence with numerals; supply a word or spell out the figures. Please note: numbers below 100 should be hyphenated when they consist of two words:

thirty-nine

V. Titles

5.1 Always include the first name or initials of persons the first time they appear in an article.

5.2 One initial should never be used; use both initials, the first name, or the first name and middle initial: J. H. Ward, John Ward, or John H. Ward, but not J. Ward.

5.3 Never use *Mr., Mrs., Miss,* or *Ms.* except in course descriptions and obituaries and in second reference to a Protestant minister. (see 5.4 and 5.11)

the Rev. James W. Byrnes—thereafter, Mr. Byrnes

the Rev. Mary White—thereafter Ms. White

Professors King and Randolph and Mr. Brown (only in course descriptions)

5.4 The word *the* should be supplied before *Rev.* in formal publications. The abbreviation *Rev.* should never be used without the first name or initials.

> Rev. Joseph T. Lehman, thereafter, Father Lehman (for a priest), Mr. Lehman (for a minister), or Pastor Lehman (for a Lutheran and clergy in some other denominations)

> Never Rev. Lehman, Reverend Lehman, J. T. Lehman, or Lehman

> Rabbi Joseph Goldberg, thereafter, Rabbi Goldberg

5.5 Use the title *Dr.* when referring to a doctor of medicine, dentistry, or veterinary medicine.

5.6 When referring to Purdue staff members, use the title or rank given them by the University, e.g., Prof. Samuel Brown, Dean Henry Frazier.

5.7 After referring to an individual by full name, use the spelled-out title and last name: Professor Smith, etc., only if the person has a professional title.

5.8 Apply the title *professor* only before the name of a staff member of professorial rank: professor, associate professor, or assistant professor.

5.9 Do not qualify the title *professor* with associate or assistant before a person's name, but do qualify it after the name.

> Prof. Samuel Brown, Professor Brown

> Samuel Brown, associate professor of biology

> For distinguished professors:

> Samuel Brown, Moss Professor of Engineering and professor of civil engineering

5.10 Avoid using long titles before the names of people, such as: Superintendent of Public Instruction John H. Ward. Rather say, Supt. John H. Ward, or John H. Ward, superintendent of public instruction.

5.11 Do not identify individuals by race, religion, or national origin unless such identifications are essential to an understanding of the story.

VI. Footnotes

Type and placement of footnotes.

6.1 If you use reference marks instead of superior figures, a new series of reference marks should begin on each page, as follows:

*	asterisk or star
†	dagger
‡	double dagger
§	section mark
‖	parallels
¶	paragraph mark

6.2 Placement of reference marks

Place after any punctuation mark, except the dash or a closing parenthesis, if the reference is made to material within the parenthesis.

Set reference marks after the word or paragraph which is explained or amplified.

6.3 Separate items in the footnote by commas, listing the information outlined below:

> Name of the author or authors (print first or given name or initials before the last name).

> Title of book, article, periodical, etc. (print title or article within a book or periodical first).

Publication data.

For a book:
> Number of the edition or volume (if there is more than one)
> City of publication
> Publisher
> Year of publication
> Page numbers of the particular citation

For a periodical:
> Number of the volume
> Number of the issue
> Month and year of publication
> Page numbers of the specific citation

Examples:
> Floyd Merrell, *Deconstruction Reframed* (West Lafayette, Ind.: Purdue University Press, 1985). p. 82.

> David A. Caputo, "Evaluating Student Cognitive Change in the Introductory American Politics Course," *Teaching Political Science* 6, no. 1 (October 1978): 23-48.

6.4 Underline titles of books and periodicals in order to indicate that italics should be used in printing.

6.5 All titles of articles, chapters, or divisions of a publication should be listed in quotation marks.

Copyreading symbols

The symbol or term	How used	Its meaning
⟋ ⟍	⁵⁄Deadline ⟍	Note the quotation marks
═	John Smith	Set in small capitals
∿∿∿	professor	Set bold face
───	Sophomore	Set in italics
'	John , James	Note comma
⊙ ✗	the end⊙ the end✗	Note period
No ¶	No ¶ The club room	Do not paragraph
¶ ⌐ ⌐	¶ The ⌐ The ⌐The	Paragraph
⌒	The room club	Transpose words
∿	club	Transpose characters
stet	book ⊷ not **stet**	Restore the text
⟩	State ⟩ street	Join separated matter
≋	Not ▓▓▓ here	Delete matter crossed out
☰	f	Make it a capital letter
⁄	✗	Make it a small letter
⊂	Pro fessor	Close up
⁄	first floor	Separate
‿	police, the station	Insert letter or word
◯	ave.	Spell out
◯	avenue	Abbreviate
◯	nine	Make it a digit
◯	9	Spell it out
⟧ ⟦	The club room is⟧ in the rear of the building, he learned. ⌐	Indent on both margins

The symbol or term	Its meaning
more (or) ↓	Story is not completed
30 (#)	Story is completed

154

Proofreading marks

⊙ Period	**CAPS** Capitals
,/ Comma	**S.C.** Small capitals
:/ Colon	**C.+S.C.** Caps and small caps
;/ Semicolon	**ITAL.** Italic
V/ Apostrophe	**bf** Boldface
V/ Quotation marks	Defective letter ✗
-/ Hyphen	Take out
(/) Parentheses	**INSERT** Insert at this point
[/] Brackets	**sp.** Space is not even
V/ Superior letter or figure	Insert space #
/2 Inferior letter or figure	Close u p entirely
‖ Align vertically	[Move to left
⊢—⊣ One em dash	Move to right]
(Circle) abbreviation to be spelled	] Center [
¶ Paragraph	**STET** Let stand all matter above dots
[2]¶ Paragraph indention 2 ems	**2]** Indent two ems
No¶ No paragraph / Run in or run on	Lower Case letter lc
Z Mark-off or break / Start a new line	**wf** Wrong font letter
Insert matter omitted — **OUT SEE COPY**	Transpose letters
	tr. word transpose

155

About the Authors

K elvin J. Arden was affiliated with Cornell University for more than 20 years as director of publications and director of communications. He also served as director of publications at New York University for a decade and began his career in college publications in 1952 at Purdue University. He has 35 years experience as a consultant on graphic communications to educational institutions and professional organizations. Arden is a graduate of North Central College and Northwestern University's Medill School of Journalism. He now lives in Cocoa Beach, Florida, and heads Arden Associates, consultants in graphic communications and book production.

W illiam J. Whalen has directed the publications program at Purdue University since 1950. He is also director of the Purdue University Press and an associate professor of communication. Whalen attended the University of Notre Dame and holds degrees in journalism from Marquette and Northwestern. Before joining the Purdue staff, he was a Navy public information officer on Saipan and Guam, a reporter and city editor, a Linotype operator, and a printer. He has authored or co-authored 12 other books and more than 300 magazine articles, pamphlets, and encyclopedia articles.

Bibliography

Arnold, Edmund C. *Arnold's Ancient Axioms: Typography for Publications Editor.* Chicago: Ragan Report Press, 1978.

_____. *Ink on Paper.* New York: Harper and Row, 1963.

Ashley, Paul P. *Say It Safely.* Seattle: University of Washington Press, 1970.

Bahr, Leonard F. *ATA Advertising Production Handbook,* 4th ed. New York: Advertising Typographers Association of America, 1969.

Baker, Stephen. *Advertising Layout and Art Direction.* New York: McGraw-Hill, 1959.

Ballinger, Raymond A. *Layout and Graphic Design.* New York: Van Nostrand Reinhold, 1970.

Beach, Mark. *Editing Your Newsletter.* Portland, OR: Coast to Coast Books, 1988.

_____; Shepro, Steve; and Russon, Ken. *Getting It Printed.* Portland, OR: Coast to Coast Books, 1986.

Better Information for Student Choice. Washington, DC: American Association for Higher Education, 1977.

Biggs, John R. *Basic Typography.* New York: Watson-Guptill, 1968.

Bonus, Thaddeus, ed. *Improving Internal Communication.* Washington, DC: Council for Advancement and Support of Education, 1984.

Burke, Virginia M. *Newsletter Writing and Publishing.* New York: Teachers College, Columbia University, 1958.

Butcher, Judith. *Copy-Editing: The Cambridge Handbook.* Cambridge, England: Cambridge University Press, 1975.

Campus Periodicals: Form Follows Function. Washington, DC: Council for Advancement and Support of Education (April 1988 CURRENTS).

Carter, Virginia L., comp. *How to Survey Your Readers.* Washington, DC: Council for Advancement and Support of Education, 1981.

Catalogues Are for Students, Too. Washington, DC: American Association of Collegiate Registrars and Admissions Officers, 1958.

Chadbourne, Bill. *What Every Editor Should Know About Layout and Typography.* Arlington, VA: National Composition Association, 1984.

Chappell, Warren. *A Short History of the Printed Word.* New York: Knopf, 1970.

The Chicago Manual of Style, 13th ed. Chicago: University of Chicago Press, 1982.

Craig, James. *Designing with Type: A Basic Course in Typography.* New York: Watson-Guptill, 1971.

_____. *Production for the Graphic Designer.* New York: Watson-Guptill, 1974.

Crawford, Tad. *The Writer's Legal Guide.* New York: Hawthorn, 1977.

Desktop Publishing. Washington, DC: Council for Advancement and Support of Education (January 1989 CURRENTS).

Flesch, Rudolph. *The Art of Readable Writing.* New York: Harper and Brothers, 1949.

Flint, Emily P., ed. *Creative Editing and Writing Workbook.* Washington, DC: Council for Advancement and Support of Education, 1979.

Halley, William C. *Employee Publications.* Philadelphia: Chilton, 1959.

Helmken, Charles M. *Great Ideas.* Washington, DC: Council for Advancement and Support of Education, 1988.

_____, ed. *Creativity Illustrated.* Washington, DC: Council for Advancement and Support of Education, 1983.

Hurlburt, Allen. *Publication Design: A Guide to Page Layout, Typography, Format and Style.* New York: Van Nostrand Reinhold, 1976.

Hurley, Gerald D., and McDougall, Angus. *Visual Impact in Print.* Chicago: American Publishers Press, 1971.

In Search of Students: Recruitment Mailings that Work. Washington, DC: Council for Advancement and Support of Education (May 1987 CURRENTS).

Jones, Gerre. *How to Prepare Professional Design Brochures.* New York: McGraw-Hill, 1976.

Kacmarczyk, Ronald, and Rickes, Persis. *The Complete College Catalog Book.* Washington, DC: Council for Advancement and Support of Education, 1984.

Keeping Your School or College Catalog in Compliance with Federal Laws and Regulations. Washington, DC: Federal Interagency Committee on Education (HEW), 1978.

Kessler, Lauren, and McDonald, Duncan. *When Words Collide: A Journalist's Guide to Grammar and Style.* Belmont, CA: Wadsworth, 1988.

Kilpatrick, James J. *The Writer's Art.* Kansas City, KS: Andrews, McMeel & Parker, 1984.

Klare, George R. *The Measurement of Readability.* Ames, IA: Iowa State University Press, 1963.

Kotler, Philip, and Cox, Keith K., eds. *Marketing Management and Strategy,* 3rd ed. Englewood Cliffs, NJ: Prentice-Hall, 1980.

Laing, John. *Do-It-Yourself Graphic Design.* New York: Macmillan, 1984.

Lasky, Joseph. *Proofreading and Copy Preparation: A Textbook for the Graphic Arts Industry.* New York: Mentor, 1954.

Lawson, A.S., and Archie Provan. *Typography for Photocomposition.* Arlington, VA: National Composition Association, 1976.

Lem, Dean Phillip. *Graphics Master 3.* Los Angeles: Dean Lem Associates, 1983.

Managing the Publications Office. Washington, DC: Council for Advancement and Support of Education (April 1989 CURRENTS).

Marson, Charlotte, ed. *How to Conduct a Communications Audit.* Washington, DC: Council for Advancement and Support of Education, 1988.

McLean, Ruari. *Magazine Design.* London: Oxford University Press, 1969.

McWilliams, Peter A. *The Word Processing Book.* Los Angeles: Prelude Press, 1982.

Melcher, Daniel, and Larrick, Nancy. *Printing and Promotion Handbook,* 3rd ed. New York: McGraw-Hill, 1968.

Miers, Earl Schenck. *Composing Sticks and Mortar Boards.* New Brunswick, NJ: Rutgers University Press, 1941.

Murgio, Matthew P. *Communications Graphics.* New York: Van Nostrand Reinhold, 1969.

Nelson, Roy Paul. *Publication Design.* Dubuque, IA: William C. Brown, 1983.

Nicholson, Margaret. *A Practical Style Guide for Authors and Editors.* New York: Holt, Rinehart and Winston, 1967.

Perrin, Porter G. *Writer's Guide and Index to English,* 4th ed. Chicago: Scott, Foresman, 1968.

Pickens, Judy. *The Copy-to-Press Handbook: Preparing Words and Art for Print.* New York: John Wiley, 1985.

Pocket Pal for Printers, Estimators and Advertising Production Managers, 13th ed. New York: International Paper, 1983.

Quick, John. *Artists and Illustrators Encyclopedia.* New York: McGraw-Hill, 1967.

Redding, W. Charles. *How to Conduct a Readership Survey.* Chicago: Ragan Communications, 1982.

Rehe, Rolf F. *Typography: How to Make It Most Legible.* Carmel, IN: Design Research International, 1974.

Reilly, Robert T. *Public Relations in Action,* 2nd ed. Englewood Cliffs, NJ: Prentice-Hall, 1987.

Responsible Editing. Washington, DC: Council for Advancement and Support of Education (October 1985 CURRENTS).

A Role for Marketing in College Admissions. New York: College Entrance Examination Board, 1976.

Rowland, A. Westley, ed. *Handbook of Institutional Advancement,* 2nd ed. San Francisco: Jossey-Bass, 1986.

Sanders, Norman. *Photographing for Publication.* New York: Bowker, 1983.

Seybold, John W. *Fundamentals of Modern Composition.* Media, PA: Seybold Publications, 1977.

Seymour, Harold J. *Designs for Fund-Raising.* New York: McGraw-Hill, 1966.

Simon, Morton J. *Public Relations Law.* New York: Appleton-Century-Crofts, 1969.

Skillin, Marjorie E., et al. *Words into Type.* Englewood Cliffs, NJ: Prentice-Hall, 1974.

Smith, Virginia Carter, and Alberger, Patricia LaSalle, eds. *How to Cut Publications Costs.* Washington, DC: Council for Advancement and Support of Education, 1984.

Stark, Joan S. *Inside Information: A Handbook for Better Information for Student Choice.* Washington, DC: American Association for Higher Education, 1978.

Strunk, William Jr., and White, E.B. *The Elements of Style,* 3rd ed. New York: Macmillan, 1979.

Swann, Cal. *Techniques of Typography.* New York: Watson-Guptill, 1969.

Tinker, Miles A. *Legibility of Print.* Ames, IA: Iowa State University Press, 1963.

Topor, Robert S. *Institutional Image: How to Define, Improve, Market It.* Washington, DC: Council for Advancement and Support of Education, 1986.

Tschichold, Jan. *Asymmetric Typography.* New York: Reinhold Publishing, 1967.

Turnbull, Arthur T., and Baird, Russell N. *The Graphics of Communication,* 2nd ed. New York: Holt, 1968.

Van Leunen, Mary-Claire. *A Handbook for Scholars.* New York: Knopf, 1978.

White, Jan V. *Designing for Magazines.* New York: Bowker, 1982.

White, Jan V. *Editing by Design: A Guide to Effective Word and Picture Communication for Editors and Designers.* New York: Bowker, 1982.

Without Bias: A Guidebook for Non-discriminatory Communication. San Francisco: International Association of Business Communicators, 1977.

Worcester, Robert L. *In Print: How to Plan, Purchase and Produce Print.* Bloomingdale, IL: Media Associates International, 1989.

Yeck, John D., and Maguire, John T. *Planning and Creating Better Direct Mail.* New York: McGraw-Hill, 1961.

Zinsser, William. *Writing with a Word Processor.* New York: Harper and Row, 1983.

Periodicals

Art Direction, 10 E. 39th St., New York, NY 10016

Chronicle of Higher Education, 1255 23rd St. NW, Washington, DC 20037

Chronicle of Philanthropy, 1255 23rd St. NW, Washington, DC 20037.

Communication Arts, 410 Sherman Ave., Palo Alto, CA 94303

Communication Briefings, 140 S. Broadway, Pitman, NJ 08071

CURRENTS, CASE, Suite 400, 11 Dupont Circle, Washington, DC, 20036

Electronic Publishing and Printing, 29 N. Wacker Dr., Chicago, IL 60606

Journal of College Admissions, 1800 Diagonal Rd., Suite 430, Alexandria, VA 22314

MacUser, PO Box 56986, Boulder, CO 80321

MacWorld, 501 Second St., San Francisco, CA 94107

Marketing Higher Education, 280 East St., Suite 114, Mountain View, CA 94043

PC Publishing, 950 Lee St., Des Plaines, IL 60016

Personal Publishing, 101 S. Gary Ave., Carol Stream, IL 60188

Print Magazine, 104 Fifth Ave., New York, NY 10011

Publish! 501 Second St., San Francisco, CA 94107

Scholarly Publishing, University of Toronto Press, 10 St. Mary St., Toronto, Canada, M4Y 2W8

Index

Admissions material 49-55
Advertising 107,127
Announcements 106
Annual fund 64
Annual reports 34,77-83,132
Architectural renderings 118
Art 115-122
Artists 8,121
Author's alterations 146
Authority, editorial 13,21

Belt presses 126-127
Bequest forms 63-64
Bibliography 159-163
Bids, composition 31
  printing 28-30,125
Biennial publication 43,127
Bills, checking 37-38
Binding 127
Bourke-White, Margaret 109
Brigham Young University 105
Broker, printing 35
Budgetary responsibilities 11
Budgets 1,3,11,15-16,79
Buyer, printing 37
Buying printing and composition 27

Calendars 100,107
Cameron belt system 126-127
Campaign publications 59-62
Campus maps 103
Career materials 49-55
Carlyle, Thomas 129
Cartoons 116
Case book 60-62

Case statement 60
Catalogs 10-11,22,39-47,131-132
Centralization 13
Color, use of 28,36,69,120-121
Committee, publications 14
Computer graphics 8,119-120
Contract, printing 29,32-33
Copy editor 8-9
Copyreading symbols 154
Copy preparation 20,142
Cost estimates 21
Costs, college 52-53
Council, publications 15
Cropping, photo 111

Design 46,115-122,124,145
Designers, graphic 8,16,35
Development publications 57-65
Direct mail 58-65,67-75
Directories 103,107
Distribution 11,99

Economy, printing 123-128
Editing, techniques of 19-26
Editorial responsibilities 10-11
Editors 5,7-8,20-21
Editors, copy 4-5,8-10
Electronic publishing, see desktop publishing
Envelopes 64,69,74,124
Estimates, printing 21,29,136,143
Evaluation 17

Facts booklets 108
Faculty handbooks 85-87
Financial aid booklets 105

Financial reports 81-82
Fitzhugh, Susie 110
Flesch formula 22,45
Floor plans 104
Fog Index, Robert Gunning 22-23
Foreign student publications 107
Four-color process 37,120-121
Franklin, Benjamin 27-28
Free-lance writers 20
Frills 24
Fund-raising publications 57-65

General information booklets 52-55
Grant proposals 62-63
Graphic designers 8
Guidebooks 104

Handbooks 85-90,116
Honesty 45,114
House organs 95-101
House sheets 126
Housing booklets 106

In-house composition 8,92,125-126
Internal communications 95-101
International student publications 107

Letters 68,72-73
Levine, Joshua 113
Line drawings 116
Living arrangement booklets 106
Logo 117-118

Mailing costs 73-74
Mailing lists 70-71,75
Maps, campus 103,117
Marketing 5
Mass media 2
Miers, Earl Schenck 7
Minority recruitment publications 106
Myers, Thomas A. 125-126
MIT 15

Newsletters 91-93,137
Newspapers 1-2
Notebooks 108

Omnibus catalog 40
Organizing the publication office 7-18
Overruns 28,146

Paper 35-36,126
Parent, Ronald 110

Parents handbooks 89-90
Parents newsletters 92
Pasteups, camera-ready 124,146
Phonathons 64-65
Photos 25,109-114
Photo services 114
Photos, sources of 114
Photographers 8,109-114
Planning sheet 12
Planning, publications 124
Policy 13
Pope, Alexander 123
Post cards 108
Postage 70,73
Postal regulations 128
Posters 105-106
Pray, Francis C. 26
Press runs 125
Print media 2
Printers, selecting 34-35
Printers 135-136
Priorities 10
Production manager 9
Production responsibilities 11
Programs 107
Proofreading 9,25,145,155
Prospectus 52-55
Publications office
    organization of 7-18
    responsibilities of 10-11
Publications, special purpose 103-108
Publicity 2
Purchasing 11,27-38
Purdue Reports 92

Radio 2-3
Readability 22-23,45-46,142
Records, production 16
Recruiting materials 49-55
Religious opportunities booklets . . 104-105
Reply envelopes 64,70
Reports, annual 77-83
Responsibilities of publications offices
    budgetary 11
    distribution 13
    editorial 10
    production 12
Review committee 15
Rooney, Andy 67
Ruskin, John 27

Schedule of classes 107
Schneihofer, Alan G. 53-55

Seal, official 117,147
Self-mailers 124
Seminars 137
Separations, color 28
Service and clerical handbooks 87
Seymour, Harold 59
Silber, John 49
Smith, Virginia Carter 67-70
Speakers rosters 104
Specialists, publications 4-5
Specifications, printing 29
Special purpose publications 104-108
Storch, Otto 115
Style, editorial 10,24-25
Style guide, sample 149-153
Student handbooks 87-89
Student interns 127

Tabloids 127
Technology, new 129-133
Telephone books 107
Television 2-3
Testing methods 17
Thompson, Bradbary 14

Thompson, W. O. 14,39
Thoreau, Henry David 72
Threshold of attention 1
Titles, academic 24
Trade customs 28
Type faces 124
Typesetting 125-126
Typographical devices 45

Underruns 28,146
University of Florida 117

Videos 133
Viewbooks 52
Visits, college day 17

Walking tour maps 103
Web offset 16-17,126
Window envelopes 70
Writer, staff 9-10
Writing 19-20,26,137

Zapf, Hermann 119-120